LOVE THAT DARES TO SPEAK

LOVE THAT DARES TO SPEAK

A five-session group study course exploring
Christian reactions to homosexuality

HILARY BRAND

DARTON·LONGMAN + TODD

the balance (from 'libra' – scales). Nearer to what we are aiming at, but also carries the idea that a clear balanced conclusion will be reached.

Dialogue, however, is rather less conclusive and therefore more complex. Coming originally from the Greek, it has its roots in the idea of gathering or collecting together. And what it gathers is words and meanings. It is about conversation, about finding meaning through words. What it is not about is aggression, or winning, or even about clear conclusions.

And neither is this course. The point of following it is not to arrive at the end with a uniform opinion or an agreed policy. Our church councils or synods may need to arrive at such conclusions, but we don't. Therefore, the expectation must be that this course will leave some people with more questions than answers. Its purpose is to shake people of all opinions out of their certainties and assumptions, and its end result is not decisions but relationships. It is about difference and the possibility of celebrating it, rather than fearing it.

In a society that has changed in areas of sexuality and relationships as drastically as ours has over the last 50 years – and that is still in a process of change – uncertainty seems to me a highly appropriate outcome. I recognise that it's an outcome many of us dislike. It's uncomfortable when things you thought were firm begin to seem shaky. But when it comes to spiritual growth then uncertainty is not only inevitable but desirable. It's when you step beyond what you thought you knew, that new virtues – humility, trust, faith, listening, waiting, learning, openness – begin to kick in. And we could all do with those.

To this end I have tried to ask questions that are not loaded, to be fair in expressing opposing opinions, and to communicate information and ideas without being directive. Clearly, I will sometimes have failed, and for that I apologise. But I hope that in participating in this course you will be able to trust the process and enjoy the journey.

HOW IT WORKS

Each week has a preliminary chapter introducing the issues to be discussed and providing background information. These will be referred to in the sessions and therefore it is important that each participant has a copy of the book and reads it beforehand and after each session.

The purpose of each session is to:

- Find out what the Bible actually says and what factual evidence is actually available.
- Share our own thoughts and experiences, and listen to those of others.
- Listen for our own feelings, experiences and prejudices – share them honestly.
- Speak and listen to God in prayer.

In order to approach the subjects in different ways, questions are asked in different formats:

- **Ask:** Finding out what you know or what a specific Bible passage says.
- **Brainstorm**: Short quick-fire answers, gathering instant responses as on a particular topic.
- **Ponder and share:** Sharing of personal experiences which may take some time to recall, so a short time of quiet should be allowed first for people to think. This is where people share from their heart and not their head and is not the place for discussion.
- **Discuss:** More controversial ideas or complex subjects that may require some further conversation.

The first two can be addressed in the whole group – if it is a large group, it may be good for some of the latter two to be tackled by breaking up into smaller groups of three or four.

Entering into conversation on some of the issues in this book will be for many people somewhat akin to entering a minefield. It would be all too easy for group members to become defensive and therefore aggressive, to talk too much or to withdraw from talking at all.

For that reason, while I would usually suggest it may be helpful for different participants to take turns in leading, in this course it is essential that the leader is a facilitator – a very specific skill. Even if you don't have anyone with facilitating experience, try to find someone with the ability and commitment to facilitate and use them throughout. (See pp. 105 – 106 in the Leaders' Notes for more information on what this entails.)

And for that same reason, before we start we need to lay down some basic principles.

SUGGESTED PRINCIPLES FOR GROUP SESSIONS

- Agree to 'suspend judgement' for the duration of the course. Do not censor or leap to conclusions.
- Set aside the need to agree or disagree or to defend your position.
- Try to be as honest and transparent as possible, including any feelings of tension. Speak as much as possible from your experience, rather than at a theoretical level.
- Actively listen to each contribution, rather than thinking about what you would like to say. Listen as well to your own thoughts and reactions.
- Respect each other's viewpoints and if possible, try and understand what formed them.

- Make it a rule that nothing said within the group is repeated outside. Make it a safe place to be honest.
- Try to build on others' ideas rather than combat them. Ask yourself 'Where does this take my thinking? What does this reveal about my assumptions?'

≈

WEEK 1

Responding to a changing world

TO START YOU THINKING

Examining my own experience

'What images or experiences do the words *gay*, *lesbian* or *homosexual* immediately conjure up for you personally?'

This question will come up in the first session, and the first important thing to say about it is that there is no right or wrong answer. Because one thing is certain, everyone approaches these words with a widely different portfolio of background images, experiences and ideas. Some of these will be conscious, rational and informed, but there will, perhaps inevitably, be others that linger below the surface, never really examined and often carrying feelings and reactions of which we are barely aware. We need to share these background experiences, not only because it will then begin to build up a bigger picture, but also because we can then begin to understand where each other is coming from. And to do that, we first need to understand ourselves.

The first thing we need to understand is that we may not be as rational as we think we are. Daniel Bohm, the physicist with a passion for dialogue who I mentioned earlier, said this:

With the aid of a little close attention, even that which we call rational thinking can be seen to consist largely of responses conditioned and biased by previous thought. If we look carefully at what we take to be reality, we begin to see that it includes a collection of concepts, memories and reflexes coloured by our personal needs, fears and desires, all of which are limited and distorted by the boundaries of language and the habits of our history, sex and culture.

So that is our first task, to bring back to mind those images, ideas and emotions that have informed our thinking.

As writer of this course, it is important that you know where I too am coming from, so I want to begin by sharing some of my own experiences, images and ideas, which I now realise are often contradictory and confused!

Go back several decades to the discovery that Salim,[2] a friend since college days, was gay. We were surprised at the time, but my husband and I enjoyed visiting him and his 'friend' Roger (the word partner was not then in general use), in their relaxed and charming home and thought little more about it. Requiring rather more thought was the discovery that another of our oldest friends and one of the most committed Christian members of our church youth group was lesbian. For her, it has been a long, painful and secret struggle to live the celibate life she believed her evangelical commitment required of her. (And indeed, at that time it did require it. Right across the evangelical spectrum there were no alternatives, no dissenting voices to be heard.) At times her journey involved breakdown and distress that was almost suicidal, but over the years it brought spiritual maturity and equilibrium. Some of this we have journeyed with her, sharing the same evangelical assumptions. We are delighted that she has eventually been able to build a home and a close and committed, but non-sexual relationship, with a very dear friend.

Go back just a decade or so, to the weekend when staying in Brighton we suddenly found ourselves caught up in the annual gay pride march. I don't for one moment suppose all such marches are like this, and probably even this one was not entirely so – we weren't able to stay long enough to find out. But the overwhelming impression of those few moments was of something menacing and disturbing. Whether it was the leather bondage gear, the intimidating drag queens, the shouting and whistle blowing, the jostling and aggressive slogans, I'm not sure, but it was certainly a disquieting experience, one that, for me, stirred up prejudice rather than challenging it. It seemed to have everything to do with promiscuity and excess, and nothing to do with love and commitment. The atmosphere also would have had a great deal to do with the release of pent-up frustration and anger for some of the participants, and perhaps I should have understood that better.

But a contrasting impression, also going back a decade or so ago comes from working for a while in the headquarters of our Anglican diocese. There I began to discover and observe from a distance some of the priests who were known to be gay. I learned of the good work they were doing, often in the most difficult inner-city areas, and heard them spoken of with respect. I read some of the writings of Jeffrey John, then at the height of his notoriety as a potentially gay bishop, and discovered how wise and spiritually discerning they were.

Fast forward to almost a year ago, when Kathy, daughter of one of my closest friends, was marrying her lesbian partner. It was a spontaneous reaction when I and several other friends from the church offered to help cater for the wedding party. We loved both mum and daughter, and again had shared a little of their difficult journey in coming to terms with the revelation of Kathy's orientation and discovering the happiness her life partner had brought her. It was an exhausting day for us, the catering 'angels', but a happy one.

Also last year, I had several long conversations with Sean, a younger friend, a highly-committed worship and youth leader in an evangelical church, in his thirties and finally coming to terms with his gay orientation and bravely journeying beyond his comfort zone to explore honestly what this meant for him and his faith. Would it mean leaving his church and his calling, and along with them all his social life and circle of friends? Did it mean abandoning his beliefs of many years, and if so what could take their place? To be true to himself, he knew he had to be willing for all these changes. But in the end, for him, following Christ as he saw it meant that most of these things would remain. He retains his evangelical position and has made the clear choice of a celibate lifestyle. But one thing is different – and different from that of my much older friend – he wants things out in the open. He wants to remain in the place he is, but to be known fully as who he is. He doesn't want to hide any more. He wants to be known as gay. I respect enormously this decision, as I also respect Kathy's choice to be married.

All of which tells you, I suppose, that I am still dealing with uncertainty. You will probably have gleaned that I have moved on from the evangelical position I once had, but neither do I see myself as a signed-up liberal, catholic, charismatic, or any other churchmanship brand. The categories no longer apply.

You will also have noticed that I've used the word 'journey' with the same annoying frequency as contestants on reality TV shows. When you find yourself involved in something life-changing, then no other word seems to do. When society's norms change around you, then standing still is no longer an option. You may emerge at your destination carrying the same beliefs and choices that you began with, but if you want to grow and develop as a person then you must travel – or shrivel!

SESSION 1

INTRODUCTION:
WHY THIS COURSE?

The wider Church's views on homosexuality have for a long time been heard mainly as aggressive opposing voices. Within local congregations, however, there has more often simply been silence.

Neither of these reactions solves the problem of how the church should respond to homosexuality. But while this controversial topic forms the central focus of this course, in practice it is about something much bigger. Because as we grapple with this one controversial issue, out of it arise many wider and deeper questions that affect every one of us:

- On what do we base our beliefs and how do we respond to a changing society?
- How do we maintain moral integrity without being judgemental?
- How do we live respectfully towards differences of opinion and lifestyle?
- How do we become as loving, challenging and inclusive as Jesus Christ himself?

To get to these wider and deeper questions, we need to look at others that are much more specific, and maybe more challenging. Therefore, it is important before starting, to understand how this course is going to work.

Look at the 'How it works' section on pp. 11 – 12. Go through the different sorts of questions and their responses and agree the basic ground rules.   *5 mins*

Ask   *2 mins*

Any questions or comments?

Brainstorm   *10 mins*

In the whole wider area of sexuality, not just gay issues, things have changed massively in our western society over the last 50 or so years. List all the many different aspects of sexuality that have changed.

One thing we see right from the start is that a vast amount of change has happened in an extremely short time. It all began to change in the 'Swinging Sixties' of course – the defining moment perhaps being 2 November 1960 when a jury declared that *Lady Chatterley's Lover*, f-words and all, might actually be 'the kind of book you would wish your wife and servants to read'.

Ask   *10 mins*

What is your era? Were your formative years in the Swinging Sixties (and if so were they as swinging as the media portrayed it)? Do your formative years go back even further and were you therefore brought up in a world of greater strictness and stigmatisation of those outside the norm?

Or do you come from a later era or a different culture, where differences were much more accepted? Go around the room with each person sharing quickly where they are coming from.

Brainstorm   *2 mins*

Looking at all the changes you've just listed, which traditional Christian views do you think they undermine?

Underlying all these societal changes is something more fundamental that we may need to grasp more fully before we go on.

Read
Genesis 1:27-28

Ask *1 min*
What was the first task of humanity as described in that passage and why is it now not such a desirable purpose?

When the intrinsic link between sex and procreation has been broken then that drastically changes the understanding of what sex is for. And before we go any further we need to realise that we are still in the midst of all this change. We don't yet know where it's all going or where it will end. We don't yet fully know what the impact of these changes will be on the next generation. There's lots we don't know about the biological or psychological roots of sexual orientation. There are so many things we simply don't yet understand. And it's important to acknowledge this.

So first, in the light of all these changes, we need to establish where we as individuals are coming from.

Ponder and share *10 mins*
What images or experiences do the words 'gay', 'lesbian' or 'homosexual' immediately conjure up for you personally?

So, we've all had a variety of experiences, and the words will conjure up a wide variety of images, some good, some bad, some stirring up prejudice, some dissolving it, some creating confusion.

And here we are in a vastly different world, and somehow we have to negotiate our way through it and seek out which, if any, of the old ways we need to retain and which can and should be left behind. Each session of the course is going to do this in a variety of ways, but now in the rest of this session we're going to go on to look at other major aspects of culture in which the church has shifted its position drastically and see what clues if any they give us.

Let's look first at one of the most recent battles that has been fought within the church: that of the role of women.

Read
1 Corinthians 14:34-35; 1 Timothy 2:11-14

It's pretty clear, if you base your views on those teachings from Paul, that many of our churches are in grave violation of biblical teaching. So why do we feel it is right to disregard them?

Ask *3 mins*
What has changed for women, in purely practical ways, since the days of Paul's teaching?

Let's look at a much older battle, that of slavery. The Bible seems perfectly happy with the idea of keeping slaves. Nowhere does it condemn it (although slave trading is denounced in 1 Timothy 1:10).

Read
Ephesians 6:5; 1 Timothy 6:1

Ask *3 mins*
So how was slavery different in the eighteenth century, when William Wilberforce campaigned against it, from what it had been in Paul's day?

Ask   *2 mins*
We've looked at what has changed practically; now, looking at both those issues, what are the underlying change in beliefs that fuelled reform?

Ask   *1 min*
Going back to our Bibles, can anyone think of any ways in which the teaching and life of Christ has fuelled those underlying changes of belief?

Although the first Christians seemed to accept the status quo of their society, and what seem to us its injustices, there are signs that things were beginning to change.

Read   *1 min*
Romans 16:1-2 (Phoebe a deacon)

Philemon verse 16 (no longer as a slave, but as a dear brother)

And then there's this marvellous counter-cultural statement in which Paul shows that deep down he understood the changes that belief in Christ was going to make.

Read
Galatians 3:27-28 (all one in Christ Jesus)

So, it seems that Paul and the first Christians understood how the message of Jesus Christ had the potential to bring huge changes to the culture in which they lived. They also knew however that their job was to set up a fledgling church within that culture, and that it was not yet the time to challenge it. Nevertheless, in subtle ways, the old ways were beginning to be undermined.

Ask   *5 mins*
We're going to end with a short time of prayer, but before
then, does anyone have any questions or comments they
are burning to bring up?

MEDITATION

Silence   *1 min*

Prayer
*Loving Lord, we recognise that we have seen many
changes in our lifetime and that fast-moving change
inevitably brings both tension and confusion. Help
us therefore, Lord, to be gentle with each other as we
negotiate living in a changing society. And help us
together to seek out what you want to say to us, and how
you want to lead us and your wider church forward with
love and compassion, challenge and moral courage,
integrity and justice. Amen*

Read
Galatians 3:27-28

Prayer   *1 min*
In a short time of quiet, pray for any individuals or
groups known to you for whom these issues of sexuality
and particularly homosexuality are particularly difficult.
Pray also for the leaders of our churches, that they may
have wisdom, courage and sensitivity.

Closing prayer (note addition)
*May the grace of our Lord Jesus Christ, and the love
of God, and the fellowship of the Holy Spirit be with
us all, and with those who we love, and with those who
struggle this night for integrity and wholeness, now and
ever more, Amen*

TO CONTINUE YOUR THINKING

Summary and Questions

- Our world has undergone a vast number of changes in areas of sexuality and relationships over the last half century, particularly regarding homosexuality. *Are we now in a position to make informed decisions about how Christian ethics should respond to these changes, or are we still in a state of flux and unable to clearly understand?*
- Some of these practical changes, particularly contraception, have seriously affected various other moral standards previously taken as givens by Christianity and Western society. *How much should we adapt our moral stance in the light of practical change?*
- The Church has changed its views drastically in the past on other social issues, for example: slavery and the role of women. *What were the underlying biblical principles that fuelled these changes and do they apply now with regard to gay issues?*

EXAMINING OUR WORLD VIEW

Read
Romans 1:18-27 (They worshipped and served created things rather than the Creator v. 25)

This passage is one of those in the New Testament to

mention homosexuality – and we will return to that aspect of it in Session 3. For now, though, let us consider the other characteristics of the society that Paul was talking about.

In this session we discovered how circumstances, often very practical ones, make big changes to culture and that these are changes that we have to grapple with. But alongside this are also shifts in beliefs, attitudes and assumptions, often for the good, but also sometimes for the bad. These underlying beliefs are often described as a worldview, the pair of intellectual spectacles through which we view the world. And like spectacles, we sometimes forget we are wearing them. Because the spectacles themselves are invisible to us, we forget that everything we see is viewed through their lenses. We don't stop to think what our worldview actually is.

Another term for the prevailing beliefs and mood of any particular period in history is the *zeitgeist*, sometimes referred to as the 'spirit of the age'. Paul clearly thinks that the spirit of his pagan Roman age is a godless and wicked one. I guess that preachers and moralisers have always thought that about the age in which they find themselves, but it is worth considering whether any aspects of Paul's era carry resonances with our own.

The first that struck me was in verse 18 where it speaks of people who suppress the truth. I'm not sure that ours is an age that *suppresses* the truth – a plethora of media old and new ensures that dissenting voices can always be heard. But, ironically perhaps, it is this very volume of opinion that has served to *devalue* truth. Not for nothing was 'post-truth' chosen as the Oxford Dictionary word of the year for 2016. It describes a trend, particularly in politics, in which 'objective facts are less influential in shaping public opinion than appeals to emotion and personal belief'; in which rationality has been replaced by knee-jerk reactions, and a sense that it's impossible to ever really get at the truth and therefore my 'truth' is as valid as yours.

The second resonance is in verse 22 where Paul describes people who have 'exchanged the glory of the immortal God for images'. Again, not for nothing is ours described as an 'image culture': one in which visual images – sometimes sleazy, sometimes seductive, sometimes aspirational – are all-pervading. Their sheer volume means they have often lost the capacity to shock. But does that mean they have lost their capacity to 'inflame lust'?

And then there is verse 25: 'They worshipped and served created things rather than the Creator' – a definition of a materialistic worldview if ever I heard one.

When we consider the rights and wrongs of the culture in which we find ourselves, we need to look closely at the practical circumstances that have shaped it, but we also need to examine the worldview, the 'spectacles' through which we are viewing it. Subjected to political 'post-truth', bombarded by images, constantly driven toward the materialism that is essential to keep the capitalist machine turning over – what are these influences doing to us? Put them together with the innate human tendency to seek comfort in anything that seems easier than a demanding and holy God, and it is easy to see how moral standards could slip drastically without us even noticing.

So then, it is easy to see how Paul's world is different from ours, but how is it the same? When we try to evaluate the rights and wrongs of any issue, including the one in hand here, then it is necessary to look at both practical aspects and underlying worldviews. This leads to hard questions and complicated answers. Therefore, we need every tool of understanding at our disposal, and it is with this that next week's study begins.

WEEK 2

Grappling with ancient tradition

TO START YOU THINKING

The four-legged chair

Some years ago, in one of our great cathedrals, full of very learned and experienced clergy, I listened to a debate on homosexuality. As an experience it was almost comical. The speakers, though implacably opposed, were scrupulously polite, but it was quickly evident that a meeting of minds was going to prove impossible. It was obvious that the arguments put forward for the two opposing sides were each based on a completely different premise. Their debating points shot past each other like a volley of misdirected arrows and, interesting as it was, the whole exercise was completely pointless.

As good Anglicans, they really should have known better.

If you know anything at all about history, you will know that the Church of England was born in the Tudor period amid a fierce battle for hearts and minds between Catholics on one side and the newly-growing body of Protestants, on the other. You'll probably also know that it involved Henry VIII, his desire for a new wife, Anne Boleyn, and his desperation for a son.

But it actually began with an artefact that came on the scene just before Henry arrived as king – the Bible printed in English. It had been translated long before this, but now these English Bibles were arriving from the continent in large numbers. People were beginning to read for themselves and to ask some difficult questions: Where do some of these traditions like penance and purgatory and indulgences come from? Why do we need priests to do it all for us? Over on the tradition side, people were fearful that religion would turn into a big free-for-all, with everyone interpreting scripture just as they felt like it.

It was an argument that was not at all polite, involving quite a few beheadings and human bonfires; the balance of power see-sawing back and forth in the short reigns of Edward and Mary, until Elizabeth I arrived on the throne and decided a bit of common sense and compromise was needed. The person who provided a rationale for this was a sixteenth-century theologian called Richard Hooker. He realised that for the English church to survive these battles it needed to lay down a middle way of understanding. This was his formula: Scripture *and* Tradition, but with Reason to balance them both out. This is what he said:

'What scripture doth plainly deliver – to that in first place credit and obedience is due; the next is whatsoever any man can necessarily conclude by force of reason; after these the voice of the Church succeedeth.'

It came to be pictured as a three-legged stool. The legs were Scripture, Reason and Tradition and without all three a balanced understanding was impossible. Without them England would have been torn apart; with them Elizabeth wisely brokered a middle way that came to be known as the Elizabethan Settlement. With them the Anglican church grew to what it is today, a broad church, based on acceptance of difference – something that is both its strength and its weakness.

Much later, in the eighteenth century, John Wesley, the founder of Methodism, claimed that the Church should add Experience to those three other sources of authority. His theory is called the Wesleyan Quadrilateral, but I shouldn't worry too much about that. Let's just assume that Experience is now incorporated as well, and that instead of a three-legged stool, we now have a rather more comfortable chair, with the four legs of Scripture, Tradition, Reason and Experience. Which, if you think about it, corresponds to the four main expressions of church we have today: Evangelical, Catholic, Liberal and Charismatic.

All this works very well, of course, if you put all these different understandings and expressions together as one. Where it fails is with the many churches and individuals who cling desperately to just one of these sources of authority, a situation ultimately as wobbly as standing on one leg.

What was happening in my cathedral experience was a debate between on one side an alliance of supporters of Scripture and Tradition, versus on the other an alliance of Reason and Experience (the latter in this case being not Charismatic but psychological and societal). It was like watching a group of people standing on one leg and then firing missiles at each other. No wonder they missed!

The point of a four-legged chair is that it only achieves balance if you put your weight on all the legs. And that is the reason for this lesson in church history at this point in the course. In order to gain a balanced understanding of the issues before us, we need to ensure that we ourselves as individuals have a good balance. To do that we first need to understand where our imbalance lies. Which of these sources of authority: Scripture, Tradition, Reason or Experience, do we consider the most important? To continue with this debate, we are going to need all four perspectives, and to listen to views from each corner.

ॐ

SESSION 2

(Welcome and reiteration of ground rules (pp. 12 – 13) and any background to course needed.)

INTRODUCTION

Last week we looked at the many changes that have taken place around sexuality over the last 50 years, in terms of both practice and belief. To consider how we might react to these we looked at previous issues on which the church has changed its view: slavery and the role of women. We saw how cultural changes since the Bible was written and in particular changes in understanding about equality have led to changing viewpoints, viewpoints in which the Church's sources of authority – Scripture, Tradition, Reason and Experience – had to be called on and yet again rebalanced.

This week we are going to remind ourselves of those different sources of authority that shape our Christian understanding and consider how each of us uses them. We will then look at what the Old Testament says about homosexuality and ask how relevant it is now, before looking at how Jesus came both to reinforce and undermine the old law and how the New Testament moves the emphasis from law to grace.

Ask
Is there anything that has come up in your thinking since the last session that you would like to discuss?

Ponder and share *4 mins*

Which of these four sources of authority – Scripture, Tradition, Reason and Experience – is most significant to you personally?

Discuss *4 mins*

What do you think is important about each of them, and conversely what might be the problems and limitations of each?

It may be that this exercise has uncovered subtle differences you were never aware of before. If so, you may realise afresh how important it is to listen and learn from each other, in order to get the balance right.

Ask

Any other comments or questions before we move on?

Now for a few quick-fire questions and then some serious Bible searching.

Ask

What do you think the Bible basically says about homosexuality – is it for or against?

Ask

How many Bible verses refer directly to homosexuality? Anyone like to guess?

Ask

What did Jesus say about gay people?

So we have a bit of a problem here, in that there really isn't a great deal to go on.

Let's look first at the story that has given a name to a gay sexual practice – Sodom.

The story begins in the first book of the Bible, Genesis 18, where three strange men visit Abraham and he offers them hospitality. Abraham identifies one of them as the Lord and the other two as angels. God tells Abraham that he is going to destroy the city of Sodom because of its wickedness. The two strange men or angels then go to Sodom where Abraham's nephew Lot is staying and Lot also offers them hospitality.

Read
Genesis 19:4-8

Ask
There are some obvious problems with this passage – what are the ones that occur to you?

The traditional understanding of this text is a prime example of how interpretations and ideas can creep in that might not have been originally intended.

The story goes on to tell us that the Lord did indeed destroy Sodom and Gomorrah, raining down burning sulphur on them. But what exactly was their sin and their wickedness? If you look elsewhere in the Old Testament, in Ezekiel, you see what people thought at that time in biblical history, about 600 years before Christ.

Read
Ezekiel 16:49

Ask
So, what do you think was the main sin of Sodom as seen at that time?

Historical research has shown that it was this view that held sway in other Jewish teaching right up until the time of Christ. When Jesus himself refers to Sodom, which he does when he sends out the disciples to the surrounding countryside, again it's very much with reference to welcome.

Read
Matthew 10:14-15

But it was about the same time that a Jewish philosopher called Philo introduced the idea that gay sex was a key ingredient of the sin of Sodom. He first argued that the root of Sodom's wickedness was in having 'goods in excess' – back to the materialism suggested as a root last week – and he then mentioned their gluttony, pleasure-seeking and lewdness. He then went on to say: 'Not only in their mad lust for women did they violate the marriages of their neighbours, but also men mounted males without respect for the sex nature ....'

By the fifth century BC, Philo's interpretation had become the more common one, for both Christians and Jews, but it wasn't until 1297 AD that the word 'sodomy' – with the specific meaning of anal sex – first appeared in the English language. And this then creates confusion in the interpretation of some other Bible verses in the King James Version published in 1611.

Read
Deuteronomy 23:17

Based on scholarship, all Bible translations from the twentieth century onwards identify this verse as being about cult prostitution, both male and female, and translate it accordingly. The King James Bible however translates it as:

'There shall be no whore of the daughters of Israel, nor sodomite of the sons of Israel.'

So you can see how translations and interpretations change and how we need to be careful in our understanding.

Let's move on now to the only other key statement in the Old Testament that is unquestionably about homosexual behaviour, and it's in that part of the Bible where all the Old Testament laws are laid out: Leviticus.

Read
Leviticus 18:22

Ask
Giving that chapter a quick scan, what other sexual prohibitions can you see?

Ask
Would we still go along with most of these?

And of course, there are a many other laws in Leviticus that don't make any sense to us today.

Read
Leviticus 11:6-7 and 10

So, no rabbit stew, no bacon, no prawn cocktail – although the penalty wasn't so great, you simply made yourself unclean. You would have been in deep trouble however if you worked on the Sabbath or uttered a curse against the Lord. Both of those could incur the death penalty, as would gay sex. In chapter 20 of Leviticus, it repeats the same statement as Leviticus 18 and states that it carries the death penalty.

All this means we have a problem about how we view these prohibitions. Obviously, some may have had practical reasons then that they don't have now, some were related to pagan ritual practice, some may have had cultural reasons, and we can also see quite a few basic moral commands we still believe to be vital.

As to which of these categories Leviticus 18:22 comes into – well, maybe that has to be for you to decide.

It may be that some of you are thinking: we're talking about really ancient writing, why does it matter to us at all? Well, one reason is that these references have never really gone away. They're still being quoted today.

Read

- In 2015, Michele Bachmann, a right-wing US congresswoman stated that God would destroy America as he destroyed Sodom and Gomorrah because of abortion and same-sex marriage.
- In 2016, Filipino boxer Manny Pacquiano quoted Leviticus 20 as against same-sex marriage – and had his Nike endorsement taken away from him for bigotry.
- In February 2017, a large sign quoting Leviticus 18 was put up outside a church near Seattle that was seen as pro-gay.

Ponder and share   *5 mins*
Why do you think it matters what the Old Testament says?

How much does the Old Testament matter to you? Do you value it and if so, why?

At the very least the Old Testament matters to us as Christians because it is the whole background to the arrival of Jesus Christ. Clearly Jesus himself referred to it and quoted it quite often. Let's look now at some of the things Jesus said about the Old Testament Law.

Read
Matthew 5:17

So that couldn't be clearer – Jesus respects the law, he hasn't come to put it aside, he has come to fulfil it. Before we look at what that means, let's see what else Jesus said about the law. He clearly respected it, but he had some angry things to say about the way the religious teachers of his day used it. Listen to these extracts from Matthew 23 and listen out for ways in which Jesus felt the law was being misused

Read
Matthew 23:1-4, 13, 23 -28

Ask
Which statements did you notice in that passage about the misuse of the law?

Ask
Can anyone remember how Jesus summed up the law in two commandments?

Read
Matthew 22:37-40

So, going back to the question we left hanging in the air earlier, about Leviticus' ban on homosexuality:

Ask
Do any of the things that Jesus said shed any light on Leviticus 18:22 and how we view it?

Perhaps this quote from Bishop Alan Wilson is a good one with which to sum up:

'The Bible needs to be taken very seriously, and literally, but then interpreted in two worlds, the one from which it came and the one in which it is applied.'

Ask
Before we move on to a short time of meditation and prayer, does anyone have any questions or comments about what we've looked at?

MEDITATION

So, Jesus understood the absolute heart of the Jewish faith: love of God, and love of neighbour.

He also understood the fulfilment he was to bring in releasing God's love to us, bringing us freedom and forgiveness. It was something that his followers could only begin to understand after his death and resurrection. Listen now to four more New Testament readings (with brief pauses between each one). Then in the silence, think about what these add to our understanding of guilt and grace, and law and freedom.

Read
Romans 10:4

Read
Galatians 3:23-28

Read
Galatians 5:4 & 13-14

Read
Ephesians 2:8

Silence

Prayer

Loving Lord, we know how often Old Testament verses, like these we've looked at today, have been used for hatred rather than love, for division rather than unity.

Lord, help us to take these words seriously rather than dismissing them, but then to see them in the light of your gospel.

Help us to reach a wise and loving understanding of how they might or might not apply today.

Help us to bring together in prayer the tools you have given us: scripture, tradition, reason and experience, and search out what you would have us believe and speak.

Help us to respect those who see things differently, and to try to understand what formed those views.

In the name of Christ.
Amen.

Quiet prayer

Let's pray now for Christian leaders and teachers – in our own church, our own denomination, our own country and then those elsewhere. Pray for those who have been schooled in bigotry, ignorance and fear. Pray for wisdom, enlightenment and courage to ask hard questions.

Closing prayer (note addition)

May the grace of our Lord Jesus Christ, and the love of God, and the fellowship of the Holy Spirit be with us all, and with all Christian leaders and teachers now and forever more. Amen.

TO CONTINUE YOUR THINKING

Summary and questions to take away

- The Church's sources for balanced thinking about truth and morality have been defined as: Scripture, Reason, Tradition and Experience. *Are you personally balanced in your spiritual thinking? Is your church?*
- In the story of Sodom, God's punishment has more to do with sins of materialism, selfishness, lack of hospitality and violence to strangers, than with gay sex. *If God were to punish our nation, what do you think would be its outstanding sins?*
- Jesus respected the Old Testament law but was also angry about its misuse, especially when it placed burdens on others. *How do you think Jesus might speak of Leviticus 18:22 to today's generation?*

READING THE OLD IN THE LIGHT OF THE NEW

Read
Galatians 3:23-28 & 5:4 & 13-14 (You, my brothers and sisters, were called to be free 5:13)

It's a glaringly obvious thought, but probably none of us twenty-first-century Christians would have heard of Leviticus were it not for the totally game-changing attitude of Jesus Christ towards it.

First, he changed it by what he said. Six times in the Sermon on the Mount comes the refrain, 'You have heard it that it was said ... But I tell you ...' (Matthew 5). He uses it with reference to murder, adultery, divorce, making oaths, revenge, and love, and in each case he is going back to the intention of the saying and pointing out that it is more than a rule. A much deeper heart attitude is needed.

And then he changed things by what he did. Sweeping away all those fussy rules about animal sacrifice: a dove for this wrongdoing and a lamb for that; by his one great sacrifice he ensured that we could be put right with God by repentance – heart attitude – alone.

So we need to read the Old Testament because the New Testament sprung from it. Themes like sin, sacrifice, forgiveness and redemption run right through the Bible like golden threads, with a gradually-growing understanding that God is not just about retribution, and holiness is not just about rules. (I'm not saying that all the Bible charts a long progress toward understanding and holiness. Often it is one step forward and one back – sometimes two back. But then if we look at the history of Christianity and indeed at the history of all religions, we would find the same. Humans, unfortunately, are like that!)

But all those weird Levitical rules were a vital step forward in their day. They were a giant leap in the understanding that for life to be good it needed to be holy. Right living was about purity in every aspect – about sex, about eating, about neighbourly relations. These rules elaborated in their own way for their own generation on a basic code that has stood the test of time – the Ten Commandments. So those sexual prohibitions in Leviticus 18 provide detailed commentary on one great simple theme: 'You shall not commit adultery'. It's a principle that has stood the test of time. Human relations work best when sex remains within a context of total commitment.

So the Old Testament deserves our respect. And what that respect deserves is that we understand the broad sweep of its intentions. Basing a theory on just one or two verses is not only intellectually lazy, it could be dangerous. As Richard Rohr provocatively suggests, 'If you read searching for certain conclusions ... as if each line in the Bible was a full dogmatic statement, all spiritual growth will not just stop, but you will become a rather toxic person for yourself and others.'[1]

Most importantly, understanding the broad sweep of the Bible means reading the Old Testament in the light of the New. Those verses from Galatians at the top of this passage are key. Paul summarises the impact of what Jesus said and did, and concludes that it makes the difference between prison and freedom, between a domestic servant and a family member, or between childhood and adulthood – 'no longer under a guardian' (ch 3 v25). Those rules were good for giving you a firm framework for life, but now you can apply reason and experience – and above all 'grace'.

(Although again a proviso: I have picked out specific verses for convenience, but please don't take my word for it. Even if you don't have time now, when you can, read it all. Take time to discover the broad sweep!)

&

WEEK 3

*Matching first-century instruction
with twenty-first-century
experience*

TO START YOU THINKING

A world away from our own

You may remember a quote mentioned last week, which also has bearing on this week:

> *'The Bible needs to be taken very seriously, and literally, but then interpreted in two worlds, the one from which it came and the one in which it is applied.'*

So, before we go further, it might be helpful to try and understand what homosexual practice Paul might have come across in his world.

In ancient Greece, a common practice was where an older man, usually married, would have sexual relations with an adolescent boy as part of a mentor relationship. This was seen as acceptable as long as the boy was the passive partner. For a man to be a passive partner was seen as shameful. The expectation was that the boy would go on to heterosexual marriage in the usual way.

In Roman culture, same-sex relationships between masters and slaves were not uncommon. The master would normally be married, and might also have sex with concubines and female slaves.

We also need to understand that although in our Timothy passage the word homosexuality was used in translation, it is actually not a word that's used at all in these cultures or in the Bible. The Greek words used are either *malakoi* meaning 'soft' or effeminate or taking a female role, or *arsenokoitai*, literally meaning 'man in bed'.

Reams have been written about these two words, and I don't want to add to the verbiage here. If you are interested, see suggestions for further reading at the back. To summarise though, the arguments are that *arsenokoitai* could have been a word invented by Paul himself – it does not appear in any earlier Greek literature, and is not the obvious one to use for the behaviour mentioned above. That would have been the Greek word: *paiderasste*, translated as pederasty today. So the meaning of *arsenokoitai* remains uncertain. Suggestions are that it could refer to predatory homosexual attacks, male prostitution, or even masturbation.

But even if it does mean that homosexuality as practice is condemned, as most Bible translations suggest, what does seem clear is that homosexuality as an orientation was either completely unknown or completely unmentioned.

So let's contrast that with our understanding of homosexuality today. Here are some quotes from Christians who have come out as gay in recent years:

- Vicky Beeching, writer, broadcaster, singer:
  'At 12 my feelings toward other girls at school began to deepen. Realising I was attracted to them was a terrible feeling. I was so embarrassed and ashamed. It became more and more of a struggle because I couldn't tell anyone... I felt there was something really wrong with me, that maybe I was so sinful and awful I couldn't be healed.'
- Jeremy Marks, founder of Courage, a Christian organisation to 'cure' homosexuality:
  'I'd known I was gay from the age of 13. I got on well with girls but I didn't feel the sexual chemistry I felt when I watched Richard Chamberlain in *Dr Kildare*.'
- Wesley Hill, Christian author:
  'By the time I started high school, two things had become clear to me. One was that I was a Christian...

The second thing was that I was gay. For as long as I could remember, I had been drawn, even as a child, to other males in some vaguely confusing way, and after puberty I had come to realize that I had a steady, strong, unremitting, exclusive sexual attraction to persons of the same sex.'

- Jayne Ozanne, Evangelical member of General Synod:

  'After many years of silent struggle, I had to find out who I was, and whether the love I craved would actually bring me the joy and peace that I so desperately yearned for. In doing so, I believed I would be walking knowingly away from the light and into the dark, turning my back on the source of all Life and Love. It's difficult to put into words how sickeningly awful this made me feel ....'

When we talk of gay issues we need to understand that these examples are the experience of most of the people we are talking about. We're talking about people who never chose to feel the way they do. Whether this was just as common in ancient cultures but quietly overlooked, or whether its apparent proliferation is something new to our generation (perhaps a kind of evolutionary mutation in the light of population explosion!), is open to debate.

There is no question that many variants of homoerotic relationships have existed throughout history and across different cultures, sometimes outlawed, sometimes tolerated, but never before part of the mainstream of societal behaviour. It seems that in the West at least, something fundamental has changed, and it is this change that we are struggling to understand.

There has been a lot of debate and research over recent years as to the roots of gay orientation, whether it lies in nature or nurture. The old suggestion that homosexuality has to do with an absent or weak father has been largely discredited. There has been some discovery of genetic difference, but this is far from conclusive. It seems the jury is still out.

And of course, there are those who deny that any shame or guilt is involved at all, that promiscuity is the new norm and that they have a right to any form of sexual expression they choose (except for paedophilia of course which in contrast has become violently demonised). There is a body of gay opinion that is actually opposed to same-sex marriage, believing that monogamy of any kind is completely outmoded. Andrew Sullivan, a conservative political commentator, who is not a Christian and is gay himself, writes this:

> 'The gay liberationists have plenty to answer for. For far too long they promoted the tragic lie that no avenue of sexuality was any better or nobler than any other; that all demands for responsibility or fidelity or commitment were mere covers for 'neo-conservatism' or worse, 'self-hatred'. They have demeaned gay men almost as surely as their unwitting allies, the fundamentalists.'

This, of course, is all part of a much wider questioning of the role of marriage, which we will examine in Week 4.

⚘

SESSION 3

WELCOME AND RECAP

Just to remind you where we've been so far in this course:

In week one we looked at the vast changes in sexuality across the board that have happened in the last 50 years, and the problems of relating Christian teaching to a changing world

Last week we reminded ourselves of the sources of authority that help us in our understanding: Scripture, Reason, Tradition and Experience. We then went on to look at what the Old Testament had to say about homosexuality, at how Jesus interpreted and fulfilled the Jewish law, and therefore how we might view it.

So this week we are going to look at what the New Testament has to say on gay issues. We'll look at the world that was coming from and at the world of gay people today, and try to understand how the two worlds do or don't match up – and indeed whether that matters.

But first, to get you thinking, a quick multiple-choice quiz:

Quiz   1 min

1. **What percentage of the UK population is gay?**
   1.5 per cent
   6 per cent
   10 per cent

2. **The incidence of HIV in the UK has steadily gone up over the last decade. In 2015 it was around 89,000 people. What do you think was the highest source of infection?**
   Homosexual sex
   Drug-use
   Heterosexual sex

3. **How many same-sex marriages took place in the 18 months since it was legalised in 2014?**
   50,000
   15,000
   5,000

4. **How many people in the UK believe same-sex relationships are 'not wrong at all'?**
   34 per cent
   55 per cent
   64 per cent

5. **How many Anglicans in the UK believe same-sex relationships are 'not wrong at all'?**
   34 per cent
   55 per cent
   64 per cent

6. **What success rate has been reported from Christian organisations that have tried to change gay orientation by therapy or prayer?**
   None
   15 per cent
   30 per cent

7. **How many verses in the New Testament refer to homosexuality?**
   None
   3
   5

8. **How many verses in the four gospels refer to homosexuality?**
   None
   3
   5

9. **How many gender options does Facebook now offer?**
   4
   58
   71

10. **How does the Roman Catholic Church refer to homosexuality?**
    An objective disorder
    A moral disorder
    Contrary to the natural law

11. **How does the American Psychological Association view homosexuality?**
    A mental illness
    A disorder
    A minority orientation

We'll come back to the answers to these later, but in the meantime let's move on to those New Testament passages. In these two from Paul's letters, notice what other activities homosexuality is lumped together with.

Read
1 Corinthians 6:9-11

Read
1 Timothy 1:9-10

Ask *1 min*
What other activities does Paul describe in these lists as wrongdoing, ungodly and sinful?

Not a lot of doubt there then, that in the bit of the Bible written by St Paul at least, homosexuality is seen as sinful.

Ask *3 mins*
Many people believe that the right reaction towards gay people is to 'Love the sinner and hate the sin'. Is this a good motto, and if not, why not?

Let's look now at the other remaining passage which is slightly different.

Read
Romans 1:21-27

Ask *2 mins*
Firstly, what do you notice about the way homosexual activity is described?

Ask *2 mins*
What does Paul describe as the roots of this behaviour?

It is certainly arguable that we live in a disordered society:

one that values created things over the Creator.

one that is flooded with imagery – much of it sexual, that surely must in its turn inflame lust.

So, could it be that the apparent rise of homosexuality in our culture is somehow the result of a disordered society?

Ask   *5 mins*
Do you see the rise in more openly gay behaviour as linked to a general godlessness, or purely a result of circumstantial changes?

Or is it just that attention is now being drawn to a human condition that has always existed, but was kept under wraps for centuries?

Ask   *5 mins*
Paul clearly describes gay and lesbian activity as unnatural.

In which ways, if any, might we describe gay and lesbian activity as unnatural?

Ask   *2 mins*
Do you see gay behaviour as a choice or an inescapable orientation?

Ask   *3 mins*
Do you see sexual preferences as clear cut or part of a continuum?

Answers to Quiz   *6 mins*

Ask   *5 mins*
The 'Start you thinking' passage for this week looked briefly at what we know about same-sex relationships in the world that these New Testament passages came from.

What differences did you notice between their world and ours?

Did these differences have any moral implications?

Ask   *2 mins*

Many people in today's culture, speaking about their discovery of the fact that they were gay, speak of the sense of shame that they felt.

What is the difference between shame and guilt? And why does it matter?

Bishop Alan Wilson suggests that once people feel shamed by their orientation, it's easy to think that whatever behaviour follows is minor. If they are stigmatized already, they may as well have something to feel really guilty about.

Let's go back now to look again at the kind of people Paul was talking about. In Romans he goes on to describe them further.

Read
Romans 1:29-31

We need to ask whether this is the sort of behaviour that characterises the gay people we know or who we encounter. And if it isn't, then that again raises the question:

Are the people Paul was talking about the same as the gay people we meet now?

And if what we are looking at now is different from what Paul was looking at then, can the same prohibitions still apply?

Catholic theologian Patrick Cheng asks, 'How can we risk punishing people if we're not even sure we're talking about the same thing?'

Nevertheless, those three verses we've looked at are pretty clear-cut and they are right there in the Bible, so the opposite question would be 'How can we risk affirming same-sex relationships if we're not sure they are okay?'

We're going to leave those questions hanging in the air, for you to think about during the following week.

MEDITATION

Let's begin with a minute of silence, where we ask God what he would have us learn and take away from today's session

Silence *1 min*

Prayer
Loving Lord, we pray for all those who are struggling to manage same-sex attractions that they did not choose or expect. We pray especially for Christians trying to understand their feelings in the light of a Lord who loves them, and to align those feelings with Christian behaviour. We pray too for those whose lust has been inflamed by images or ideas, or by the predatory behaviour of others. We pray for those for whom sex has become an addiction and who are pushed toward behaviour they know to be wrong.
In the name of Christ, Amen

Quiet prayer *2 mins*
Let's pray specifically for those who feel their sexual orientation is at odds with their faith. Let us pray too for parents of gay and lesbian children, as they too often struggle with feelings of shame and guilt and confusion.

Closing prayer (note addition)
May the grace of our Lord Jesus Christ, and the love of God and the fellowship of the Holy Spirit be with us all, especially those who are struggling to align their sexual orientation with their faith. In the name of Christ, Amen

TO CONTINUE YOUR THINKING

Summary and questions

- The three references to homosexuality in the New Testament all come from the apostle Paul and occur within lists of general immorality. *Can we risk affirming something that even a small number of Bible verses describe as sin?*
- Homosexual practice in Paul's day was very different from today. Homosexuality as an orientation appears to be unknown, or certainly unspoken of. *Can we risk denying people of gay orientation the chance of loving relationships if we're not even sure the Bible is talking about the same thing?*
- Romans chapter 1 roots gay and lesbian practice in a general spiritual disorder of worshipping created things and images rather than the Creator. *Could the apparent rise of homosexuality today be linked to a general spiritual disorder or should it not be described in terms of a disorder at all?*

THE EARLY CHURCH'S BIG RISK

Read
Acts 11:4-17 & 15:6-21 'God did not discriminate between us and them' 5:9

The apostle Peter had been praying, but in the midst of it had either fallen asleep or let his mind drift into fantasy.

What happened in his state of trance was bizarre – he saw a sheet full of animals lowered from heaven and heard a voice 'Get up, Peter, kill and eat.'

Since this linen-wrapped menagerie included creatures such as pigs and camels, lizards, buzzards and owls, Peter, being a good Jew, protested. He had never eaten anything unclean and he wasn't going to start now. God's answer was unequivocal – 'Who are you to call it unclean if I'm telling you it's clean?'

Immediately after that Peter had some unexpected visitors, sent by a very unexpected person: Cornelius a Roman Centurion, a good man who'd been searching for God, but who of course, was a Gentile, a non-Jew, and therefore not someone who Peter thought could be saved by Jesus.

Not unless he became a Jew of course. But when Peter went to meet Cornelius, something very remarkable happened, not just to Cornelius but to all his household too. It was something Peter recognised. 'The Holy Spirit came on them,' he explained. It was exactly what he and the other disciples had experienced on the day of Pentecost, they were praising God and speaking in tongues. How come this could happen to people who the rest of the Jewish religion considered unclean? But then Peter remembered his dream, and concluded that something so remarkable was happening that he had to give way to it. 'If God gave them the same gift he gave us who believed in the Lord Jesus Christ, who was I to think that I could stand in God's way?'

Of course, this didn't change the fledgling church right away. If you move on to chapter 15 of Acts, you'll see that they convened a council of all the Christian leaders in Jerusalem to thrash out the issue. And there they finally agreed that yes, putting Peter's evidence with that brought back by Paul and Barnabas from their travels, there was no doubt that the Christian message was for more people than just the Jews. And jolly good too, because otherwise 2000 years later, you and I and 2.2 billion other people in the world might not be where we are now, living in the freedom and forgiveness of God's grace.

But the point of the story is this: Peter and the early Church drew on all these sources of authority: Tradition, Scripture, Reason and Experience; in order to discern what God was telling them.

There was the Old Testament tradition of the Law, the bedrock of their Jewish faith. It was immensely precious to them and they weren't going to throw it over lightly. From that they understood how important it was to stand pure before God.

But they also had Scripture – or at least, for them it wasn't written down yet, but they had the words of Jesus that Peter had heard direct from Jesus' own mouth. They had heard Jesus say that he didn't come to abolish the law but to fulfil it. They had heard that Jesus said that it wasn't what went into people's mouths but what came out that made them unclean. And they were beginning to understand that it was Jesus' death and resurrection that had cleared the way for them to become fully clean and right before God, in a far deeper way than any amount of religious law-keeping.

And then they had had experience, both spiritual and practical. There was Peter's amazing dream, coupled with Cornelius's amazing calling, and the way the Holy Spirit fell upon his entire household. It's important to remember that it wasn't just the experience of one person at one time, but all the other experiences all the original disciples had been having, as chronicled in Acts, starting with the response they'd experienced on the day of Pentecost and much more, and then including the astonishing evidence that Paul, the newcomer to the team, was bringing back from all over the place.

And so, to evaluate all this, they called on reason. They weighed up the hard evidence of changed lives.

They discussed it thoroughly, they weren't afraid to disagree. And out of all that came a decision that was a huge and ridiculous risk at the time, but turned out to be exactly the path that God wanted.

WEEK 4

*Re-evaluating marriage –
and celibacy*

TO START YOU THINKING

Small world, big implications

Perhaps the biggest underlying problem in all the
church's squabbling about homosexuality comes down
to just one little word – marriage. Respecting gay people,
accepting their committed partnerships is one thing, but
'gay marriage' – that's quite another! To an extent I
share that view; I'm inclined to think sticking with the
word 'partnership' might have been more appropriate –
and certainly less confrontational! (But then I also think
the term might be a useful option for many heterosexual
couples. Indeed, what could be more absurd and unequal
than not allowing mixed-sex couples in the UK to enter
into civil partnerships?) But the term 'gay marriage' is
out there now, and we must deal with it.

So, before we perpetuate the squabble ·any further,
let's go back and ask the question, what does the word
'marriage' actually mean? What did it mean in biblical
times, what has it meant through history and what does
it mean now?

First, you might be interested to learn that the legal
requirement in this country for any sort of formal
marriage ceremony did not exist before 1753. Second,
that marriage as a sacrament of the church only really
came on the scene in 1549 with the publication of the
first Book of Common Prayer. And third, that in Jesus'
day no public ceremony in the synagogue existed either.

There was in Jesus' time a contract to be entered into,
and, as his attendance at a marriage party (John 2) and
his story of the wise and foolish virgins (Matthew 25)

indicate, there was a public celebration.

But in Bible times, both in Jewish and Roman society, marriage had much more to do with alliances between families than just two individuals. It was also very much about property and inheritance, this too being arranged by the families.

Paul's instructions that husbands should love their wives seems obvious to us, but many of its original readers might have been surprised to see it. Marriage then was pragmatic and dynastic and not really a matter of the heart.

And so, it usually was through most of history and across most of the world. Women were handed from fathers to husbands and had few rights of their own. Indeed, women in the UK were effectively still seen as under their husband's control right up until 1882. Only then, when the Married Woman's Property Act allowed them to possess and control property in their own right, did they really gain a separate legal identity.

Since then, of course, things have changed rather rapidly. The year 2014 was notable, not only as the year that same-sex marriage in Scotland, England and Wales became legal, but also as the year when forced marriage was criminalised in the UK. Whilst arranged marriages are still legal if both partners are fully consensual, marriage can no longer be arranged regardless of the wishes of the partners, a practice that had gone back to prehistory and is still prevalent in many parts of the world today.

And ironically, at the very time when gay couples are celebrating their right to wed, marriage as a formalised institution is being disregarded very rapidly indeed by heterosexual couples. A British Social Attitudes survey in 2014 revealed that the proportion of people who agreed that 'couples who want children ought to be married' was 37 per cent, while those who disagreed numbered 34 per cent – a statistic that NatCen Social

Research who did the survey described as a tipping point.[1] They also found that 74 per cent thought there was little difference between being married and living together, while a previous survey revealed that only 11 per cent thought sex outside of marriage was 'always or mostly wrong'.[2]

It comes as no surprise that these statistics are accompanied by plummeting religious affiliation: 53 per cent now identify themselves as without religion[3] while of those who do see themselves as either belonging to or being brought up in a religion, 56 per cent never attend services or meetings and only 14 per cent attend weekly.[4]

Curiously, however, it seems marriage is still what a vast majority of people want. A 2014 survey commissioned by *The Observer* found that when asked whether they believed monogamy to be desirable, 92 per cent of people answered yes.[5]

So perhaps what these statistics show is that we should be grateful to gay couples for keeping the flame of marriage alive! Certainly, the data shows that assumptions can no longer be made about what marriage is. It's evident that what we may see as a traditional church perspective doesn't provide all the answers. It seems that the old patterns aren't working, and we may need to rethink. But it's also evident, to those of us who still cling on to Christian faith, that within its tenets lie the tools to make marriage work: love, trust, commitment, forgiveness, second chances, spiritual strength. And remarkably these tools also seem to work in the context of less conventional relationships, complex relationships and even damaged and broken ones. We should not be surprised that the spirit of Jesus brings its healing and renewing work wherever people humbly ask for it.

⚘

SESSION 4

So far in our sessions we've been talking exclusively about same-sex relationships – as if these were the most burning issues in the area of human relationships today. But are they?

They may be the most talked about, but are they the ones that cause the most pain or the most confusion? Are they the ones that most need fixing, or even the ones that have changed most over the last 50 years?

We're going to broaden our horizons in this session and consider the wider landscape of human sexuality.

Ask   *3 mins*
If we take a wider look at sexuality and human relationships in the 21st century, what do you think are the other areas that may have gone awry, or need re-examining in the light of change?

We're going to begin with the area of marriage, partly because it's the one that most affects us.

Even if we aren't married ourselves, most of us are the children of marriages, or at least of broken ones.

And going back to our theme, we can't begin to evaluate same-sex marriage, unless we first understand what marriage actually is.

Can it still be what we understand as traditional Christian marriage – and how traditional really is that? Does marriage need to be re-understood or re-invented?

Let's go back first of all to absolute Bible basics.

Read
Genesis 1:27-28a; 2:20b-25

Ask
What does it mean to be one flesh?

It could be a poetic description of the sex act: two human bodies joined as one.

But more practically it describes the outcome – a new human being whose DNA is irrevocably made up of those two individuals.

So, this brings us back to one of the questions of our first week.

If sex no longer inevitably involves creating a new life, then does that change the whole meaning of the sex act, and does it therefore change the whole meaning of marriage?

Discuss   *2 mins*
Is marriage designed primarily around having children, or is it valid on its own terms even if children don't come into it? What are the purposes of marriage other than procreation?

Discuss   *5 mins*
If having children is no longer an inevitable outcome, then is having sex outside of marriage still such a problem? Think of couples you know who are 'living together' or did so before marriage?

In your observation, has this been a problem or not?
Is there any value in trying out both sex and daily living
with someone before commitment?

Discuss   *10 mins*
'Sexual union always has spiritual consequences,
whether for good or ill.'

Do you think this is true?

This is what Jeffrey John says about marriage:

> 'Almost all of us hope for someone who will be
> there for us and who will stay with us until death
> do us part. From a specifically Christian point of
> view, this model of human loving is best not only
> for practical reasons, but because a covenant of
> this kind between two people … is in the image of
> God's own covenanted, constant love for us. It is
> sacramental because it helps make God's own kind
> of love visible in the world.'

Read
1 Corinthians 6: 18-20
The quote about all sex acts having spiritual consequences
also came from Jeffrey John, quoting this passage from
Paul. Let's see what he says:

Read
> For Paul, sexual union always has spiritual
> consequences, whether for good or ill. Promiscuous
> activity involves desecration of the body, which is a
> temple of the Spirit and itself a member of the Body
> of Christ...
>
>   Observation of what happens, both on the gay
> scene and on the straight scene, leads me to believe
> very strongly that the Church's wisdom in advising

men and women to confine sexual activity to permanent faithful relationships remains as wise as it ever was. On the firmly empirical basis of having picked up the pieces of too many damaged people, I am convinced that 'anonymous' or recreational sex is never unproblematic, or irrelevant to a person's emotional or spiritual health. On the contrary, quite apart from the guilt and fear that are usually involved, like other addictions it dulls the appetite for normal life, and creates a peculiar kind of introversion, a sense of inner exile which is ultimately destructive of real relationships. Paul's statement that sexual activity divorced from loving commitment 'tears away' part of the person, whether one wills it or not, is a matter of experience, not theological theory.

Note that he uses the word 'addiction'. This is clearly a major problem in our era and is massively influenced by online porn.

Let's move on now to what Jesus has to say. We're aware by now that he had nothing to say about gay relationships and not really anything about casual sex, but some very firm statements about adultery and about divorce.

Read
Matthew 5:27-32

Read
Matthew 19:3-9

There are almost certainly quite a few divorcees in your church and some who are remarried, and the purpose here is not to make anyone feel bad about themselves. There are all sorts of reasons why this happens; some people may feel they carry some guilt, others may not. Either way, there is no one in your group or your church who is without sin in human relationships, and therefore no one should be ready to 'cast the first stone'.

But we do need to look closely at what really mattered to Jesus. So, let's go back to the principle we've used in previous sessions of examining the consequences of divorce in Jesus' world, and the consequences now.

Ask
What if anything has changed since Jesus' day? Why might the consequences be different?

Ask
What hasn't changed?

Clearly in Jesus' firm statements on divorce he was addressing some very real issues of justice. But equally clearly, he believed that commitment was enormously important.

And as he goes on to say elsewhere, for him what happened to children was enormously important too.

Read
Matthew 18:5-7.
'Better to have a millstone hung round your neck than to cause a child to stumble.' That's fierce and pretty drastic.

Ask   *3 mins*
We're going to move on now to the subject of singleness and celibacy, but before we do so, does anyone have any questions or comments on the ground we've covered so far? There are all sorts of ways of causing a child to stumble and simple emotional neglect is probably by far the biggest one.

But one that's seen as enormous in today's culture is, of

course, child sex abuse. Which leads us on to our next subject, that of celibacy, because nowhere has child sex abuse been more publicised and more hated than in the Roman Catholic Church, a church that demands that its priests be celibate. Press and public have been quick to make the link between the sin and the celibacy.

Ask *3 mins*
In view of all the recent scandals regarding Roman Catholic priests, do you think celibacy is desirable or even possible?

Ask
What was the main difference between celibacy in the medieval period and celibacy today?

When we return to the main debate, it's important not to be drawn into the spirit of the age so much that we believe celibacy is simply not an option. Both Jesus and Paul were celibate, and they both appear to believe that being celibate is not only possible, but might actually be preferable.

Read
Matthew 19:9-12

Read
I Corinthians 7:8-9; 32-35

Ask *1 min*
What do those verses suggest are the benefits of being single?

Ask *1 min*
What do you think are the benefits of being single?

Ask *1 min*
And what are the losses – and the dangers?

Wesley Hill is a gay Christian who has chosen to remain celibate, and he has written a book to describe his experience that it is possible for a non-practising, but still desiring, homosexual Christian to live out and celebrate the grace of Christ in a celibate life. Nevertheless, he is deeply aware of his loss.

Read

> 'The longing isn't mainly for sex ... It is mainly for the day-to-day small kind of intimacy where you wake up next to a person you've pledged your life to, and then you brush your teeth together, you read a book in the same room without necessarily talking to each other, you share one another's small joys and heartaches.'

So, while it may be possible for gay people to remain single and it may even be beneficial, does the Christian Church have the right to demand it? And does it even have a reason to do so?

One placard held up in a gay rights protest asked this: 'Explain it to me again – exactly why is my gay marriage a problem for you?'

Jayne Ozanne, a lesbian member of the Church of England Synod, asks the same question:

> 'What conceivable harm is done by two people of the same sex entering into a relationship, which they hope and pray will be lasting, covenanted and monogamous, in the same way as a couple of the opposite sex?'

We're not going to discuss that now. Rather, we're going to leave it hanging in the air as a question to think and pray about during the coming week, and to come back

to in the next session. As you think and pray consider
the background to marriage outlined in this week's
introductory chapter and ask yourself how the word
'marriage' might best be used in the context of today's
complex relationships.

MEDITATION

Listen to Wesley Hill again:

Read
'What if I had a conception of God-glorifying faith,
holiness and righteousness that included within it
a profound element of struggling and stumbling?
What if I were to view my homosexual orientation,
temptations and occasional failures not as damning
disqualifications for living a Christian life, but rather
part and parcel of what it means to live by faith in a
world that is fallen and scarred by sin and death?

Gradually I am learning *not* to view all of these
things as confirmations of my rank corruption and
hypocrisy. I am instead slowly but surely learning to
view that journey – of struggle, failure, repentance,
restoration, renewal in joy, and persevering, agonised
obedience – as what it looks like for the Holy Spirit to
be transforming me on the basis of Christ's cross and
his Easter morning triumph over death.'

Wesley Hill is writing these words in the context of
homosexuality, but they could just as easily have been
written for single heterosexuals or for married people.
Because in all these areas many of us have profound
struggles, temptations and sometimes failures. We all
live in a world that is fallen and scarred by sin. For none
of us is it allowable to act on all the sexual attractions we
feel. In a time of silence now bring your own struggles to
the Lord, or those of others who are close to you

Silence 1 min

Now widen your focus and in silence bring to the Lord others known to you who are damaged by marital breakdown, or by not having the life partner they so desire. Bring to the Lord also those children known to you who are damaged by parental conflict, emotional neglect or sexual abuse. Bring also those adolescents and young people known to you as they navigate their way through a world filled with promiscuity and sexual temptation.

Silence 1 min

Prayer
Loving Lord, we know that you are with us in all these deep struggles of life.

We know that you long to comfort and strengthen those who struggle but who don't know that you are there for them.

We know that your grace is sufficient for all our needs, and that you came not to condemn but to bring redemption and love.

Help us to accept that grace, to discover that redemption and to pass on that love and grace and acceptance to all others who struggle: gay or straight, single or married.

Closing prayer (note addition)
May the grace of our Lord Jesus Christ, and the love of God and the fellowship of the Holy Spirit be with us all and with all those we love and with all those who need it. In the name of Christ, Amen.

TO CONTINUE YOUR THINKING

Summary and questions to take away

- Homosexuality is only one small area in a much wider set of issues about sex and marriage. *Do we make too much fuss about it at the risk of ignoring much bigger problems?*
- Committed loving relationships are always healthier than promiscuous ones. Jesus set a very high value on the importance of marriage commitment. *But what exactly is marriage and has it changed in the light of contraception?*
- Celibacy is not only possible but may be a good life choice. *Nevertheless, is it something we should impose on others?*

THE HUMAN PROPENSITY TO FAIL

Read
2 Corinthians 4:6-9 (We have this treasure in jars of clay – verse 7)

'What if I had a conception of God-glorifying faith, holiness and righteousness that included within it a profound element of struggling and stumbling?'

That question from Wesley Hill might well be turned around: *'Why don't I have* a conception of God-glorifying faith, holiness and righteousness that includes within it a profound element of struggling and stumbling?' Because surely that is what being a follower of Jesus means.

In those verses in Corinthians Paul is pointing out that even though we may have received spiritual light and life, they are housed within a rather crude and fragile container – our minds and bodies. It is the nature of being human to feel hard-pressed, perplexed, persecuted and struck down – and not always from without. Often these pressures come from within ourselves.

The author Francis Spufford wrote a book, *Unapologetic*, subtitled: *Why Christianity makes surprising emotional sense*. He tried to do away with the old religious cliché words and so instead of 'sin' used a rather clumsy acronym, HPtFTu, which stands for 'the human propensity to f*ck things up'. It's probably not a definition that's going to catch on in churches, but it is accurate. We do all mess up, sometimes very badly, most of the time. And maybe it's no accident that the f-word is involved, because often it is our sex lives that cause the most struggles and stumbles.

A survey in 2014 found that one in five people questioned hadn't had sex in the last month.[6] How accurate those statistics are is somewhat open to question, since according to them vastly more men than women are having sex! But looking beyond them, the likelihood is that the proportion of sexually unsatisfied people out there may be far higher than one in five. The question was only asked about one month, but of course for many of those people it was a long-term or permanent state. For many, not just gay people and not just single people, there isn't a choice – a celibacy they didn't choose has been forced upon them. Perhaps by lack of a suitable partner or loss of that partner, by pressure of work or childcare, by geographical separation, or by ill-health. And even for those who are having sex, it's not always easy. Is your partner really satisfying you, are you still desirable, where did all the thrills go, why is it getting so stale and boring, why does it seem to cause so many arguments?

In short, what I want to say here is this: look, none of this stuff is easy! It's incredibly hard and all too often we get it wrong. The effort to please a partner sexually sometimes becomes too much. The temptation to stray sometimes becomes overwhelming. Frustration often boils over into anger. All of us are sometimes weary, selfish, insensitive, cruel. Most of us are terribly inept at communicating honestly what we feel. It's very easy for commitments to be made by two people who really aren't right for each other. Marriages do fail. Vows of celibacy do prove too hard to keep.

We're all as clumsy and fragile as jars of clay, trying to hold together, but sometimes breaking catastrophically apart. And that's where being a follower of Christ *should* be our salvation. We *should* find compassion, not condemnation, we *should* discover redemption, not retribution. We may need to shoulder some blame, but we *should not* be subject to shame.

We all know the Christian Church is not always like that. Often it seems the latter of those alternatives that are most in evidence. But it need not be so. Because it's in the first of those pairs of opposites that the Christian gospel is unequivocally rooted. It's a belief system designed for the benefit of sinners. It's made for those who f*ck up. It's about grace. So don't let anyone ever tell you otherwise. And make sure you cut all the other sinners around you a bit of slack!

❧

WEEK 5

*Recreating a welcoming
and respecting Church*

TO START YOU THINKING

Heart-searching in high places

When it comes to looking at reactions to same-sex relationships in the Christian Church as a whole, it becomes rather difficult. This book can't hope to chart all the deep heart-searching and occasional procedural shenanigans that this issue has provoked in high places. I'd imagine that only the most hide-bound or other-worldly Christian denominations have been immune from such debate in recent years, and it would be incredibly difficult, not to mention boring, to try and chart those that have taken place. So, in this brief run-down, I will focus mainly on the denomination I know best and the one with the highest profile in the UK: the Church of England, with brief forays into controversy within Roman Catholic and Evangelical camps. So, just to get you up to speed, in case you aren't an avid follower of church politics:

THE ANGLICANS

The first Anglican statement on homosexuality to really hit the headlines came in 1991 with the publication of a statement from the House of Bishops *Issues in Human Sexuality*. Here, as you might imagine, it reiterated the party line, but concluded:

'The Church has begun to listen to its homophile brothers and sisters and must deepen and extend that listening, finding through joint prayer and reflection a truer understanding and the love that casts out fear.'

The listening, and sometimes the failure to listen, rumbled on for some time, but things came to a head in 2003 when Jeffrey John became the first Church of England priest, openly living in a gay relationship, to be nominated as a bishop. Despite his statement that the relationship was celibate, the ensuing controversy meant that he was pressured to withdraw his acceptance of the post. Since then he has reportedly been considered, but turned down, for seven diocesan bishoprics.

And all the while the Church has continued its rather fudged attitude toward gay clergy – what has been described as a 'Don't ask, don't tell' policy. This was a policy originating in the US military, where it was forbidden to discriminate against closeted gay people, whilst also barring openly gay or lesbian people from military service.

Jeffrey John is deeply critical of the sort of double standard that this policy brings about. He tells how when the 1991 document came out, 'a number of bishops contacted their gay clergy to assure them it didn't mean what it said'! And he continues, 'Most clergy who have taken the risk of being open with their bishops about being in a gay relationship have found support – but only in private. In public the backing is almost always withdrawn.' 'This is', he says 'a disaster for the Church's mission, its integrity and its morale.'

We need to understand, however, that there is a bigger reason for all this guardedness and lack of plain speaking. The Archbishop of Canterbury is not only head of the Church of England but of the Anglican Communion worldwide, and there are far more Anglicans outside of the UK than inside, the largest proportion being in Africa.

And there, opinion is very different. Homosexuality is illegal in at least 30 sub-Saharan African countries, and as recently as 2014 even harsher penalties were introduced in Nigeria and Uganda. Nigeria is the main focus of Anglican problems. Not only is it the fastest-growing province in the Anglican Communion, it is also a nation that is 50 per cent Muslim. So it is at the centre of a battle for hearts and minds between Christian and Muslim. The criticism that Muslims throw at African Anglicans is that by associating themselves with the sexual mores of America and Europe, the Church has become compromised, weak and in moral decline.

So, behind the Church of England's battles over gay issues is a much larger global struggle to keep the Anglican Communion together. Back in 2003, when John's nomination was still making the headlines in the UK, in the USA, Gene Robinson, an Episcopalian priest openly living in a gay relationship was elected as bishop in New Hampshire. Robinson had been married with two daughters, but came out as gay and divorced amicably in 1986, entering into a gay relationship in 1987. Despite being eligible to attend, Robinson was not invited to the 2008 Lambeth Conference for Bishops in the Anglican Communion.

Some critics have said that the Anglican Church is simply politicking over these issues, trying to hang on to global power. On the other hand, many in the Church of England feel that these links with our Anglican brothers and sisters around the world are precious and it would be a great loss if the Anglican Church were to break apart.

So the debate continues. In February 2017 the General Synod of the Church of England ended in some disarray when a majority rejected the latest proposal from the House of Bishops. The Bishops' document on Marriage and Same-Sex Relationships, basically concluded that the Church's doctrine should not change to accommodate same-sex relationships. The vote against it was seen as a victory for the pro-same-sex marriage lobby, although some of the opposing side may have voted against it as being too accommodating in its tone towards gay people.

Later in 2017, however, the Scottish Episcopal Church, also a member of the Anglican Communion, voted in favour of allowing same-sex marriage.

THE EVANGELICALS

In 2013, Steve Chalke, undoubtedly the UK's highest profile evangelical leader, sent shockwaves through Britain's evangelical community with a public statement supporting same-sex monogamous relationships. Chalke, a Baptist minister, also runs the Oasis Trust, one of the UK's largest charities running education, housing and healthcare projects, and is a well-known writer and broadcaster. In 2014 the Evangelical Alliance, representing over 4000 churches and organisations across 79 denominations in the UK, officially distanced itself from Chalke by expelling the Oasis Trust from its membership. It did comment however that it remained 'deeply respectful of the work and achievements' of the Trust and that it had 'a strong desire to avoid any unseemly dispute and to speak well of each other'. Chalke has since gone on, in 2016, to officially offer same-sex marriage in his church, Oasis Waterloo in London.

Also in 2014, Christian musician Vicky Beeching announced that she was a lesbian, adding that, 'I feel certain God loves me just the way I am'. This might not have been such big news were it not that Beeching, who is British but a big name on the evangelical contemporary music scene in the USA, was also close friends with Katharine, daughter of Archbishop of Canterbury Justin Welby. In 2015 Beeching noted that since coming out she felt unable to attend evangelical churches because of the reaction, and also that bookings for performances in the USA had totally dried up.[1]

THE ROMAN CATHOLICS

In an impromptu press conference on a plane returning to Rome from Rio in 2013, Pope Francis made a surprising conciliatory statement: 'If a person is gay and seeks God and has good will, who am I to judge him?'

In 2015 Krzystof Charamsa, a Polish priest working in the Vatican, caused a stir when he came out as gay with his partner at his side. He said, 'I want the Church and my community to know who I am: a gay priest who is happy and proud of his identity. I'm prepared to pay the consequences, but it's time the Church opened its eyes, and realised that offering gay believers total abstinence from a life of love is inhuman'. He was immediately suspended from the priesthood.

In 2016 in a document entitled 'The Gift of Priestly Vocation', the Vatican reaffirmed that it cannot admit to holy orders those who 'practise homosexuality' or support 'gay culture'. The Catholic Church is not about to change.

THE REST

Quakers have long been ahead of the game, stating as far back as 1963: 'It is the nature and quality of a relationship that matters … the same criteria seem to us to apply whether a relationship is heterosexual or homosexual.' By 2009 they were actively campaigning for legal same-sex marriage. But then Quakers, despite their roots, no longer identify as specifically Christian.

In July 2016 the United Reform Church became the

first British Christian denomination to approve same-sex marriage services, at the discretion of each individual church.

Also, in 2016 the Methodist Church in Britain voted to 'revisit' its position on same-sex marriage, with a task group reassessing its theology due to report back in 2018.

And that's it for the time being.

SESSION 5

At the end of last week's session, we left two questions hanging in the air. The first on a placard held up at a gay rights protest read: 'Explain it to me again – exactly why is my gay marriage a problem to you?' The second from Jayne Ozanne, a lesbian member of the·Church of England Synod, asked almost the same question: 'What conceivable harm is done by two people of the same sex entering into a relationship, which they hope and pray will be lasting, covenanted and monogamous, in the same way as a couple of the opposite sex?'

Ask
Is it the same question? What is the difference between the two?

Ask   *3 mins*
What, if anything, makes you uncomfortable about the idea of same-sex marriage? Is it the word or the concept, or both?

Ask   *3 mins*
What, if anything, makes you uncomfortable about the Church's attitude towards gay and lesbian people?

Today's study looks at the Church's reaction to same-sex marriage and gay partnerships – firstly at the wider Church and then at your own church congregation to ask how both can become more welcoming and loving.

A major issue in the Anglican debate is the Church's rather fudged attitude toward gay clergy – what has been described as a 'Don't ask, don't tell' policy.

Ask   *2 mins*
Is the 'Don't ask, don't tell' policy a sensible compromise or inherently two-faced? What might be the benefit of using it? And what is the down side?

Ask
On which continent are the greatest numbers of Anglicans – Europe, Africa or the USA? (If you are in a different denomination, what might you guess for that?)

Ask   *1min*
What difference might this make to any pronouncements the Archbishop of Canterbury might make? (What difference might worldwide demographics make to your own denomination?)

Ask   *2 mins*
*'Like a mighty tortoise, moves the church of God,
brothers we are treading where we've always trod.'*

The Church is generally accused of moving too slowly. What are the benefits of moving slowly and what are those of moving faster?

Ask   *3 mins*
How important do you think it is to try and keep the Anglican communion together?

Do you think it is even possible? Might there come a time when division could even be fulfilling God's purpose?

Ask *3 mins*
To what extent do we look to our Bishops or other church leaders for guidance on moral issues? Do you personally like to have a moral stance laid down for you, or do you prefer to have freedom to make up your own mind?

Ask *5 mins*
If you were the Archbishop of Canterbury, how would you deal with the gay crisis in the Church of England and in the Anglican Communion? (If you are in a different Christian denomination, and were the person in charge, how would you deal with these issues there?)

Hopefully, your answers to the last question will at least have made you grateful that you don't have to run the Church!

3 mins
Let's take a step back now from looking at the wider Church and these specific issues, and think about our own personal reactions to people who are different from ourselves, by looking at some of the things Jesus and the New Testament writers had to say.

Read
Matthew 7:1 ('Do not judge lest you be judged')

It's interesting to note that both the Archbishop of Canterbury, Justin Welby, and Pope Francis have been quoted as publicly asking 'Who am I to judge?', when questioned about their reactions to gay people. Nevertheless, both have upheld traditional church teaching.

Ask *2 mins*
How might they be modelling a way forward?

Read

Matthew 25:35 ('I was a stranger and you welcomed me in')

Author Philip Yancey quotes someone as telling him: 'As a gay man I've found it easier to get sex on the streets than to get a hug in church.'

Ask   *1 min*

What might stop you giving the gay man a hug?

Read

1 John 4:18 ('Perfect love drives out fear')

Most of us are afraid of what we do not fully understand and most of us are afraid of change. Learning to love those we don't fully understand is one step forward, accepting that we are safe in the love of God is another.

What aspects of these areas of human sexuality make you feel uncomfortable or anxious?

Read

James 1:19 ('Quick to listen, slow to speak')

After the General Synod of February 2017 again failed to agree about marriage and same-sex relationships, the Bishop of Southwark, Christopher Chessun wrote this:

> 'I believe there is scope for us to be braver and bolder in generous love and forbearance ... The key, as so often, will be to speak well of one another and to listen well... This is generous, humble listening, that makes the voice of the other have more weight than one's own.'

Jesus suggests we not only need to listen, but to watch too.

Read
Matthew 7:15-20 ('By their fruits you will know them.')

Read
Galatians 3: 26-29 ('You are all children of God ... You
are all one in Christ Jesus.')

Jonathan Berry, a gay Christian, writes that, 'Defining
our identity can be complex and confusing. Is it rooted
in gender, class, vocation, ethnicity, religion, sexual
orientation or political allegiance? ... Rather than having
a single identity, people have several overlapping
identities, which shift in emphasis in different life
stages and environments.' And he goes on, 'If we allow
our sexual orientation to define us, then we risk being
victims of spiritual identity theft.'

Ask
What do you think are the key principles that we need
to observe?

We're drawing to the end of the course now, and as we
do, let's take some time quietly to think back over where
it has taken us. After a time of quiet, each share your
reactions.

Ponder and share   *10 mins*
What have you learnt during this Lent course that you
will take away with you?
What difficulties or questions remain for you to think
over?

MEDITATION

Prayer
*Loving Lord, We pray for our church structures, for
those who lead and guide them both in this country and*

worldwide. Help them to listen, to others and to you, help them to be honest and open, and to allow others to be the same. We pray for the local congregation of which we are a part. May it be an inclusive community, willing to welcome all who come to us, determined not to label or to pre-judge, but to seek out what value and riches every human made in the image of God can bring to us.

Read

'What if the church were full of people who were loving and safe, willing to walk alongside people who struggle? What if there were people in the church who kept confidences, who took time to be Jesus to those who struggle with homosexuality? What if the church were what God intended it to be?'

The anonymous gay person who wrote those words longed so much to find that community – that place where he or she could feel safe, loved and respected. Maybe he or she is even now hovering on the fringes of your congregation, maybe even now about to walk away in disappointment. Could you be the person to welcome them in?

Read
Pope Francis:

'The thing the church needs most today is the ability to heal wounds and to warm hearts. It needs nearness, proximity. I see the church as a field hospital after battle ... Heal the wounds ... The ministers of the church must be ministers of mercy above all.'

In a time of silence, ask God if there is anything else God wants to say to you now.

Silence

In a brief time of open prayer now, as many as feel able bring to God a short statement of your hopes or challenges at the end of this course.

Open prayer

Closing prayer
May the grace of our Lord Jesus Christ, the love of God and the fellowship of the Holy Spirit be with us all, and with all gay and lesbian people everywhere. In the name of Christ, Amen

❦

TO CONTINUE YOUR THINKING

Summary and questions to take away

- The main hurdles for agreement in the Church of England are the use of the word 'marriage' for gay relationships and the 'Don't ask, don't tell' policy toward gay clergy. *What, if anything, as ordinary church members, might we do to try and resolve these issues?*
- The Church of England in particular is in a difficult position trying to keep not only its own members together, but the Anglican Communion worldwide. *Is it possible to authentically follow the example of Jesus Christ by sitting on the fence? What is the difference between loving tolerance and shallow compromise?*
- We need to acknowledge both our lack of understanding and our discomforts and fears. *What steps can we take to work through both of these?*

NOTHING PERSONAL

Read
Romans 12:9-10 (Honour one another above yourselves v10)

I wonder what your conclusions were as a group on finishing this course? It was not written with a view to pushing you to an agreed set of principles. Rather it was to open up honest discussion, with an expectation that at the end of it, opinions may still be divided. Just as they continue to be in the Church at large.

In a letter sent out after the Synod debate in 2017, Archbishops Justin Welby and John Sentamu said this:

'In these discussions, no person is a problem or an issue. People are made in the image of God. All of us, without exception, are loved and called in Christ. There are no "problems", there are simply people called to redeem humanity.'

But come on, Archbishops, aren't you being a little naive? Within our churches there are, as we know all too well, persons who make problems for us! Just as there are in our families and our workplaces and our neighbourhoods.

Other people always make problems for us – because that is the nature of personhood – each individual is different, and sometimes profoundly so. But note that little phrase 'for us' – because that is the nub of the matter. The problems that other people make for us – can be 'for us' because that is also the nature of growth. The problems are there to help us grow.

If only that made it all hunky-dory and fine. It doesn't. Growth can be bruising, bewildering and sometimes breaking. It may involve drastic pruning, the splitting of roots, transplanting to a new place, grafting onto new stock. It may involve a seed falling to the ground and 'dying'.

Because, to continue my garden analogy, the problem may lie with the other: crowding me out, taking my sunshine, sucking me dry; but then again, the problem may lie with me. Maybe I'm having that effect on others. The problem with other people may not only be 'for us', it may also be 'in us'.

And then again, the problem may not be with the

other person or with me, rather the place in which we find ourselves – environments that are arid, toxic, too small, too bleak, too overgrown, simply the wrong sort of soil. Institutions cause problems too.

But enough with the gardening metaphors! At the heart of it the Archbishops are right. No person is a problem. Each is a living, breathing image of the Almighty. Each brings God to me.

So how am I to live alongside these God-breathed, God-loved people who annoy me so much?

In our diocese another letter arrived after that February Synod in 2017. It came from our Bishop of Southwark, Christopher Chessun. In that debate, he had been the only Bishop to abstain from voting. He did it, he said, not to stake out his distance from the other Bishops, rather to mark the fact that the discussion is not over. The listening process must still go on. And this, he said, is the way to do it: 'The key, as so often, will be to speak well of each other and to listen well ... This is generous, humble listening, that makes the voice of the other have more weight than one's own.'

Really? Speaking well of someone you fear may hurt others? Allowing an opinion one feels to be profoundly wrong to be heard above your own? Acknowledging that the person you despise might actually have something to teach you.

I want to say that all this is not only idealistic, but also impractical and unwise. But then I know that the whole of the Christian gospel is full of paradoxes like this, and I also know, from long experience that, amazingly, when I allow them space in my life, they seem to work.

Archbishop Justin Welby has a frequently-used phrase to describe the sort of Anglican Church he wants to see: 'unity in diversity'. The key to this he described in 2016 as 'finding ways to disagree well'. It's a remarkable phrase, turning all the accepted norms of hierarchical established religion on their head.

But I hope that this course has been to you an exercise in that sort of discovery. I hope it has been for you an exercise in: 'finding ways to disagree well'. If it hasn't, because you have found yourselves agreeing and understanding one another much more than you thought, then so much the better. But if it hasn't, because you have found yourselves disagreeing badly, then do not despair because you have made a beginning.

The play *Oslo* by J. T. Rogers, charts the genesis of the Oslo Peace Accords signed by the Israelis and Palestinians in 1993. The process was brokered by an unlikely character, a Norwegian sociology academic called Terje Rød-Larsen, who passionately believed that any agreement would not be found simply by winning points and battling out compromises around a conference table, but by a model he called gradualism, moving on very slowly from one tiny agreement to larger ones and building a bond of trust along the way. It was a model that took time and patience. But the key to Larsen's method was not what happened in the conference room, but what happened outside it. In the play, the delegates gather in a Norwegian manor house, where Larsen tells them:

'You are here because you know that your people cannot go on as you have. That whatever you personally feel, you wish to find a way forward. But to overcome hatred and fear, pragmatism is not enough ...

Here we are all friends. While we are together, this will be our one unbreakable rule. *(Pointing to a shut door)* In that room, when the door is closed, you will converse. Disagree. Worse. But out here we will share our meals, talk of our families and light the fire. My friends, I must insist upon this rule. For it is only through the sharing of the *personal* that we can see each other for who we truly are.'

And it was in that way, in seeing the other as a person with hopes and dreams and fears like their own, over endless coffees, waffles and cigarettes, that a road map to peace was eventually drawn. No, of course, it did not then all go smoothly. It was not all solved. But it was a beginning. At the end of the play, Larsen says:

> My friends, do not look where we are; look behind you. There! See how far we have come! If we have come this far, through blood, through fear – hatred – how much further can we yet go? *(Points ahead)* There! On the horizon. The Possibility. Do you see it? Do you? *(He waits, stares at the audience)* Good.' *(The curtain falls.)*

Jesus looked at the rag-tag bunch of people around him and saw possibilities. He saw illiterate fishermen as religious leaders, women as full participants in the kingdom, corrupt quislings as models of restitution, Roman oppressors and Samaritan separatists as spiritual seekers.

So, may we learn to see each other with the eyes of Jesus and the Church as a place of cheerful and enjoyable diversity.

$\mathcal{L}$

LEADER'S NOTES

WHO SHOULD LEAD?

Because of the issues involved, this course requires not just a leader, but a *facilitator,* and that is a very specific skill. I would suggest therefore that the same person, someone with the ability to facilitate dialogue, and the commitment to do so, leads throughout.

The key attribute for a facilitator is that it is someone *impartial.* Or failing that, someone who is prepared to put aside their opinions for the duration of the course and lead in a strictly impartial manner. It means not having any agenda to push forward, rather it means trying to maintain balance and give equal weight to different opinions and allow for the fact that there may not be a clear outcome. It requires someone who doesn't feel uncomfortable with difference, rather someone who enjoys it and can defuse tension in a relaxed and good-humoured way.

A facilitator is above all someone who is gifted in listening – paying attention to what *isn't* said as much as what is, and noticing who *isn't* speaking as well as who is. It means being prepared to ask supplementary questions to draw out what someone is trying to say, or what might lie underneath what they appear to be saying. It may mean reflecting back to someone what you think they have said, but *not* summarising what you think they should have said! It may also mean allowing the room to sit in silence for a while, or to draw back and bring controversy to God in prayer if necessary.

It also means fully digesting the factual information in these leaders' notes, and being able to bring it in when necessary, whilst *not* bringing in your own slant or perspective. (It might be useful in the Ponder and Share question on p. 23 in Session 1, to share a little of your experience, but if you do so, make it entirely clear that that is what you are doing, and then leave it on one side thereafter.) For more advice, the following is a useful resource: https://diversity.missouri.edu/education/handouts/facilitating-dialogue.pdf.

GENERAL COMMENTS

This course is quite tightly crafted – deliberately so, since these are subjects that require careful statements and questions. This means there is not much scope for wandering onto other subjects. However, if there is anything that people are really desperate to discuss, it needs to be fitted in. I have tried to put a general 'any questions or comments?' section within each week. Be aware that people may want to bring in other things. If necessary schedule these things for the following session.

In some sessions there is a lot of material to be read out. To vary the voice, try to get different participants to read longer quotes. Many of the Bible references will be found in the Relevant Bible Passages in the Appendix. However, if you want to get people to look them up in their own Bibles, I find that a good way to do it quickly is to give out Post-it notes, each with a different Bible reference on, to different participants so that they can have it looked up and the place marked ready beforehand. It may be too time-consuming to wait for everyone to look up every reference. If participants don't all want to bring their own Bibles, make sure you have some ready.

If sessions are run with the question slots within the times I suggest, then each could fit within an hour, but I am assuming that they will more often spread to an hour and a half, or even two hours.

Depending on the size of your group and the space available, I would suggest that it may work best to have a short section in the middle of each session, where people divide up into threes or fours to discuss maybe two or three questions. In a larger group, it tends to be a small proportion of the group who speak, whereas in smaller groups, everyone will feel happy to pitch in. I have suggested which questions work best for these smaller groups in notes for each session. Bear in mind that you may well want to have some feedback into the larger group when they come back together, and you need to schedule time for this. Be aware that some people find it difficult to hear in a room with others talking, so spread out into different rooms if you can.

One way of mixing people up and ensuring that small groups are not composed only of people who always talk to each other, is to number them off beforehand. Decide how many small groups you want (e.g. 4) and then go around the room getting people to say their number (eg: 1, 2, 3, 4, 1, 2, 3 ...). Then direct all 1s into one space, all 2s into another space, etc.

One way of doing refreshments is to serve them at this point, so people get their refreshments as each small group comes to a natural lull.

SESSION 1

What are the different aspects of sexuality that have changed over the last 50 years?
It may be a good idea, if possible, to appoint a scribe and write these things up on a flip chart
For suggested aspects, see Timeline in the appendices.
Main issues:
The pill, abortion – sex outside of marriage, increase of cohabitation
Concerns over over-population

Homosexuality decriminalised, civil partnerships, same-sex marriage

Which traditional Christian views do these changes undermine?
Marriage for life, no sex outside marriage,
Role of women, gay activity seen as immoral

What was the first task of humanity as described in Genesis 1:27-28 and why is it now not such a desirable purpose?
Be fruitful and increase in number – population explosion.

In the beginning the sacred purpose of the union between men and women was that of bringing forth new life. If the human race was to survive it was essential. They needed to go forth and multiply. They also had no choice. Sex was inevitably linked to procreation. So here we highlight the absolute basic difference of our generation, firstly a practical rather than a moral one. It is now possible to have sex without creating a new life. And not only is it possible, for the survival of humanity it is preferable. A rapidly-growing population is no longer good for survival. Going forth and multiplying is no longer such a great idea in an earth that can no longer sustain it.

What images or experiences do the words 'gay', 'lesbian' or 'homosexual' immediately conjure up for you personally?
Allow a few moments of quiet for participants to think about this before sharing.
If a large group, then divide into threes or fours. In this case, you may wish for members of small groups to then share with the wider group when they reconvene. In which case, allow more time.

What has changed for women, purely in practical ways, since the days of Paul's teaching?

Women no longer constantly pregnant,

Menstrual periods no longer the handicap they once were

Domestic appliances and ready-made food mean home-making much less arduous

Women have economic freedom, no longer property of men

Above all, women educated

How was slavery different in the eighteenth century from what it had been in Paul's day?

In the biblical era:

There was no secure paid employment as we understand it

Most people worked on their own plot of land, had a specific trade like carpentry or fishing, or were merchants.

Unskilled workers were paid on a daily rate, a very insecure mode of life (as described in Matthew 20:1-16)

Slavery was much more like being 'in service'

Slaves were sometimes given high status, or allowed their freedom

In the eighteenth century:

Slaves were of a different race and were treated as sub-human

They had suffered the injustice of being stolen and transported to begin with

The large number of slaves per white owner necessitated a brutal rule of fear

Looking at both those issues, what is the underlying change in beliefs that has fuelled reform?

The belief that all are equal

How has the teaching and life of Christ fuelled those underlying changes of belief?
Jesus treating women and people of different races as fellow humans
Clear that gospel is for everyone

SESSION 2

Introduction
Check whether participants have read the introductory chapter, and if not, outline what it says, or get those who have read it to do so.

Which of the four sources of authority is most significant to you personally?
What is important about each of them, and what might be the problems and limitations of each?
If you have a large group then it is probably best to put these two questions together and to divide into threes and fours to discuss them. You may wish to get feedback from the small groups when the session reconvenes. In which case, remember to add extra time for this.

How many Bible verses refer to homosexuality?
Just six or seven verses (one repeats itself)
This makes 0.002 per cent of the Bible
(With a further 5 referring to male or female prostitutes at pagan shrines)
In contrast, verses on economic justice make up 10 per cent

What did Jesus say about gay people?
Nothing at all.

What are the obvious problems first encountered with the story of Sodom?
Firstly, it is obviously about gang rape rather than one-

to-one consenting homosexual activity.

Secondly, the rather troubling implication that it's perfectly acceptable to offer your virgin daughter to be raped, rather than your guest.

What was understood as the main sins of Sodom in the writings of Ezekiel?

Arrogance and lack of hospitality.

What other sexual prohibitions can you see in Leviticus 18?

With your mother, sister, aunt or granddaughter (v1-16)
With a woman and her daughter (v17)
With a woman during her monthly period (v19)
With your neighbour's wife (v20)
With an animal (v23)
It also prohibits child sacrifice (v21)

Why does it matter what the Old Testament says?
How much does it matter to you? Do you value it and if so, why?

It is probably a good idea to again break up into small groups for these questions, and allow extra time for feedback to the wider group if necessary.

Try and draw out what passages in the Old Testament people do value as important to them.

Which statements in Matthew 23 speak about misuse of the law?

Used to load burdens on others (v4)
Used to keep people out of the kingdom (v13)
Insistence on trivia while big things: justice, mercy and faithfulness neglected (v23)
More concern about outside than inside (v25)
Hypocritical (v27)

SESSION 3

Quiz answers

1. **What percentage of the UK population is gay?**
   Correct answer: 1.5per cent
   In 2013 the Office for National Statistics found that 1 per cent considered themselves gay or lesbian, and 0.5 per cent bisexual. The figure goes up to 2.7 per cent in the 16-24 age group and to 2.5 per cent in London.
   This is lower than the Government estimated in 2004 when they were considering the tax implications of Civil Partnerships, when they put it at 6 per cent
   In the 1940s the Kinsey report in the USA suggested that 10 per cent of the male population was homosexual, and many gay organisations are still championing this much higher percentage.

2. **The incidence of HIV in the UK has steadily gone up over the last decade. In 2015 it was around 89,000 people. What do you think was the highest source of infection?**
   Correct answer: Heterosexual sex. Statistics are:
   homosexual sex 47.1 per cent; drug use 2.2 per cent; heterosexual sex 48.2 per cent. A third of those infected were black Africans.

3. **How many same-sex marriages took place in the 18 months since it was legalised in 2014?**
   Correct answer: 15,000.

4. **How many people in the UK believe same-sex relationships are 'not wrong at all'?**
   Correct answer: 64 per cent

5. **How many Anglicans in the UK believe same-sex relationships are 'not wrong at all'?**

Correct answer: 55 per cent. (Source: NatCen British Social Attitudes survey 2017)

6. **What success rate has been reported from Christian organisations that have tried to change gay orientation by therapy or prayer?**

   This isn't straightforward. A survey of the results of Exodus member groups in 2006 claimed a 15 per cent 'success' rate, but this included those who reported a 'substantial reduction in homosexual attraction' rather than a clear-cut change in orientation. In 2013 some of the key leaders of organisations in the US and the UK repudiated previous claims that orientation could be changed. Exodus International, an interdenominational 'ex-gay' Christian umbrella organisation ceased functioning in that year, though some of its member organisations continued.

   In July 2017 the Church of England General Synod passed a motion condemning conversion therapy and calling for it to be banned.

7. **How many verses in the New Testament refer to homosexuality?**

   Correct answer: three. The three references all come within lists of immoral behaviour in Paul's letters.

8. **How many verses in the four gospels refer to homosexuality?**

   Correct answer: none.

9. **How many gender options does Facebook now offer?**

   Correct answer: 71. Facebook does not publish a formal list, but since it offered the option to choose your own gender identity, the number has risen to 71. These include such terms as: gender fluid, trans-sexual, trans-gender, bi-gender, poly-gender, hermaphrodite, intersex, gender queer, gender variant, gender neutral, two-spirit. Oh yes, and male and female.

10. **How does the Roman Catholic Church refer to homosexuality?**
It uses all three terms: an 'objective disorder' is used to describe gay or lesbian orientation; a 'moral disorder' and 'contrary to the natural law' are used to describe gay sexual activity.

11. **How does the American Psychological Association view homosexuality?**
Correct answer: a minority orientation. It stopped using the term 'disorder' in 1975.

What other activities does Paul describe in his lists in Corinthians and 1 Timothy as wrongdoing, ungodly or sinful?
Corinthians: sexually immoral, idolaters, adulterers, thieves, the greedy, drunkards, slanderers, swindlers.
1 Timothy: murders (especially mother and father), sexually immoral, slave traders, liars, perjurers

Is 'Love the sinner and hate the sin' a good slogan when used in relation to gay people? If not, why not?
Good – in that it differentiates between the orientation and the act.
Bad – in that most homosexual people see their sexual need as integral to who they are.
Therefore differentiating between act and person is meaningless.
Also bad – in that it automatically defines a gay person as a sinner.

What do you notice about the way homosexual activity is described in Romans 1?

Verse 26: Only verse in Bible mentioning lesbian activity

Verse 26-27: The phrases 'exchanged natural relations for unnatural ones' and 'abandoned natural relationships' carry an implication of choice.

Verse 27: The phrase 'inflamed with lust' implies promiscuity

Verse 27: Does the phrase 'received in themselves the due penalty' carry an implication of sexually-transmitted disease as an outcome?

What does Paul describe as the roots of this behaviour?

Verse 21: They did not glorify or thank God

Verse 23: They 'exchanged the glory of God for images' – allusions to our twenty-first century 'image culture'?

Verse 25: 'Worshipped and served created things rather than Creator' – allusions to materialism?

Verse 26: Therefore God gave them over to shameful lusts' – lust as the product of disordered society?

If you have a large enough group to divide into smaller groups, then the following four questions might usefully be grouped together for small group discussion. Remember to allow enough time for feedback when the full group reconvenes.

Do you see the rise in overt gay behaviour as linked to godlessness, or a result of circumstantial changes?
Here it might be worth referring to the idea of a continuum as outlined below and the question of bisexuality. This of course might be further confused by people who are basically heterosexual fantasising about or experimenting with homosexual behaviours, which

in previous societies would have been far too taboo for them to even consider.

In what ways, if any, might we describe gay and lesbian activity as unnatural?
Morally disordered, a disability, simply unusual or uncommon.

Do you see gay behaviour as a choice or an inescapable orientation?

Do you see sexual preferences as clear cut or part of a continuum?
The continuum idea was first put forward by Alfred Kinsey in his research into sexuality in the 1940s. It understands sexuality as ranging from exclusive attraction to the opposite sex to exclusive attraction to the same sex at either end of the spectrum with different degrees of attraction in between. In the 1970s Fritz Klein explored the idea further in his Sexuality Grid, which allowed for difference between understood sexual orientation as an 'ongoing dynamic process' throughout life.

Debate about these ideas continues, with recent research from Washington State University suggesting that there is a categorical difference between people who are homosexual and those who are not.

Issues of sexual preference are not to be confused with those of 'gender fluidity', since the gender which someone identifies as may not directly relate to their sexual preference.

In other words, there's still a lot of confusion out there!

What differences did you notice between the world of the New Testament and ours? Did these differences have any moral implications?
In both Greek and Roman cultures of the day, same-sex relationships were never equal, in the way we might

understand gay relationships today. Both involved a degree of power and domination. They were relations that fostered inequality rather than equality.

Nor was there any understanding of people being exclusively gay. It was always seen as a choice, an add-on to marriage, and therefore always adulterous.

What is the difference between shame and guilt?
Shame is a general feeling of being unworthy or unclean
Guilt is a bad feeling occasioned by a particular action, behaviour or thought
Guilt can be good in bringing someone to repentance and new behaviour
Shame can be something imposed by an institution or brought about by the sin of others

SESSION 4

What are other areas of sexuality and human relationships that have gone awry?

Child sex abuse
Sex before marriage
Adultery
Wider family and friendship
    relationships
#metoo

Transgender
Serial monogamy
TV portrayals
Online networks

What is the purpose of marriage other than procreation?
Mutual help (see Genesis 2:18)
No shame in nakedness (Gen 2:25) – someone who knows you fully
Safe context in which to fulfil sexual urges
Committed relationships lived in context of broader family

Is having sex outside marriage still such a problem?
Is there a need to highlight the difference between casual
    sex and unmarried committed relationships?
But can they be clearly defined?

**What if anything has changed regarding divorce
since Jesus' day?**
Jesus' day:

- divorce only the prerogative of men
- women economically dependent on men
- women had no rights to fight their cause
- women could be left destitute and deprived of their
  children

Our day:

- law requires division of assets
- women can be economically independent
- law normally allows access to children by both parties

What hasn't changed?
Children always affected
Always emotional and spiritual consequences
Sense of failure and mistrust
Wider family and friends always affected

**In view of scandals regarding Roman Catholic
priests, do you think celibacy is desirable or even
possible?**
It is important to stress here that any connection between
celibacy and child abuse is far from proven.

**What was different about religious celibacy in
medieval times?**
The celibate lived together in same-sex communities as
monks and nuns.
They were not deprived of close relationships and were
overseen by others

Four things that are interesting to note:

- The risk of child abuse by celibate priests is nothing new. In the seventeenth century in Catholic schools in Italy, they had a rule that priests were not to be alone with boys.
- There is no evidence that priests are more inclined to child abuse than any other profession. It could be that they get massively more publicity.
- There is no evidence that homosexual men are more inclined to child abuse than straight men.
- True paedophilia, as a condition, is an attraction to pre-pubescent children and it's the young age that is the focus, not necessarily whether they are male or female.

What do Jesus and Paul suggest are the benefits of being single?

- Jesus: for the sake of the kingdom of heaven
- Paul: undivided devotion to the Lord.

(Incidentally, may be worth flagging up 1 Corinthians 7:5 – the idea that married couples abstain from sex for a while to 'devote yourselves to prayer')

NB: Jesus' comment that 'Not everyone can accept this word, but only those to whom it has been given' is doubly ambiguous. First, it is not clear whether it applies to what he has just said about divorce or what he goes on to say about celibacy – though the latter seems most likely. Secondly what does he mean by 'those to whom it has been given'? The term 'eunuch' literally means a man who has been castrated. When Jesus acknowledges that some may be born that way, he could be referring to 'intersex' people: those born with a physically ambiguous sexual identity, or those with a naturally low sexual drive, those who are identified as effeminate – or perhaps gay. More well-known in Jesus' world was the concept of those made eunuchs by others – a common practice in royal courts where slaves would be castrated with the purpose of making them more reliable personal servants. Unable to have a family of their own, they could be safely perceived to have no other allegiance, and with no sex-drive, they could safely perform personal functions for the ruler (the origin of the word means 'bed-keeper' – an attendant in the bedchamber), or in and around the harem. This creates another ambiguity in the word because it is often used to mean a person of great authority and responsibility in a court – a chamberlain or chancellor – and it is in this context that the word is used in Acts chapter 8 when Philip meets the Ethiopian eunuch.

SESSION 5

What is the difference between the two questions?
The first uses the contentious word 'marriage', the second doesn't.
The first asks the question 'Why is it a problem to *you*?', to which the answer might be 'No, it isn't really my business'. The second asks a more generic question: ' Does it do harm?', to which considering society as a whole, the answer could conceivably be 'Yes'.

On which continent are the largest numbers of Anglicans?

Africa   43 million+ (20 m of which in Nigeria) (growing)
Britain 2.6 million (declining)
USA   2.2million
(80 million worldwide)

The largest numbers of Roman Catholics:

Latin America	483 million	41.3%
Europe	277 million	23.7% (declining)
Africa	177 million	15.2% (growing)
Asia	137 million	11.7%
North America	85 million	7.3%

(Source: BBC News 2013 http://www.bbc.co.uk/news/world-21443313)

Evangelicalism as a movement is of course split into many different groups, mostly with leadership within national boundaries, so the same pressures do not apply

How might the Archbishop of Canterbury and Pope Francis be modelling a way forward?

Acknowledging that they don't know all the answers, and that they too are sinners.

NB: Whilst both have publicly upheld church teaching, both have worked to shift attitudes from within.

What have you learnt during this Lent course? What difficulties or questions remain?

If possible, try to encourage each participant to answer this question.

If necessary remind participants to listen carefully and reflect on what they have in common as well as what views still separate them.

REFERENCES

WEEK 1

1　All names have been changed to protect the identities of those concerned.
2　The trial under the Obscene Publications Act was against Penguin Books for publishing an un-expurgated edition of the book. The chief prosecutor famously asked if *Lady Chatterley's Lover* was 'the kind of book you would wish your wife or servants to read'.

WEEK 2

1　Richard Rohr, *Things Hidden: Scripture as Spirituality* (SPCK, 2008), p.12.

WEEK 4

1　2016 http://www.natcen.ac.uk/news-media/press-releases/2016/may/attitudes-to-marriage/
2　2014 http://www.bsa.natcen.ac.uk/latest-report/british-social-attitudes-30/personal-relationships/marriage-matters.aspx
3　2016 http://www.bsa.natcen.ac.uk/media-centre/latest-press-releases/bsa-34-record-number-of-brits-with-no-religion.aspx
4　2013 http://www.bsa.natcen.ac.uk/latest-report/british-social-attitudes-28/religion.aspx
5　https://www.theguardian.com/lifeandstyle/2014/sep/28/british-sex-survey-2014-nation-lost-sexual-swagger
6　https://www.theguardian.com/news/reality-check /2014/jan/24/how-many-people-havent-had-sex quoting National Survey of Sexual Attitudes and Lifestyles.

WEEK 5

1 https://www.premier.org.uk/News/UK/Vicky-Beeching-I-don-t-feel-comfortable-in-evangelical-churches

APPENDICES

&

APPENDIX 1

Timeline: Setting the scene of the sexual revolution

1950s Tampons widely commercially available
1960   *Lady Chatterley's Lover* trial
1961   Contraceptive pill available
       Pre-marital sex
       Cohabitation rather than marriage
1967   Abortion Act (termination up to 24 weeks legalised)
1967   Homosexuality decriminalised
1968   *Hair* musical opened in London
1969   Divorce reform act
       (no proof of fault required – divorce after 2 years separation if mutual, 5 if one partner)
1970   First gay pride march in London (150 people attended; in 2015 1 million people attended)
1970s Concerns about overpopulation (India sterilization drive in 1970s; China: one child policy 1979)
1972   Masturbation declared 'normal' by American Medical Association
1976   Gay Christian Movement formed (became Lesbian and Gay Christian Movement in 1987)
1980s Emergency Contraception became available (the morning after pill)
1981   AIDS epidemic began
1983   50 per cent of UK population thought homosexual practice 'always wrong', 70 per cent of Anglicans
1991   Marital rape recognised

1992 Internet began

1992 Ordination of women in Church of England

2003 Jeffrey John controversy

2004 Civil Partnership Act

2004 First gay bishop (in sexually active partnership): Gene Robinson in USA

2013 Leading evangelical Steve Chalke announced support for gay partnerships
(In 2014 Oasis Trust, Chalke's charity, was expelled from Evangelical Alliance)

2014 Forced arranged marriage made illegal

2014 Same-sex marriage legalised in Scotland, England and Wales

2014 Homosexuality still a criminal offence in 81 countries

2015 73 per cent of UK population think homosexual practice acceptable, 50 per cent of Anglicans

2016 First bishop in Church of England, Nicholas Chamberlain, Bishop of Grantham, came out as gay (though in celibate relationship).

2017 Bishops' report on Marriage and Same-sex relationships rejected by C of E Synod

APPENDIX 2

Relevant Bible passages

Marriage
Genesis 1:27-28
Be fruitful and multiply

Genesis 2: 24
Man leaves his father and mother and is united to his wife and they become one flesh

Matthew 19:5
Genesis verse quoted by Jesus in context of divorce

Sodom and Gomorrah
Genesis 19:4-5, 24
All the men from every part of the city of Sodom – both young and old – surrounded the house. They called out to Lot, 'Where are the men who came to you tonight? Bring them out to us so that we can have sex with them'.

Ezekiel 16:49
A reference to the sin of Sodom: '*arrogant, overfed and unconcerned; they did not help the poor and needy. They were haughty and did detestable things before me.*'

Matthew 10:14-15
Jesus refers to Sodom in terms of lack of welcome

Jude 7
Sodom and Gomorrah gave themselves up to sexual

immorality and perversion. They serve as an example of those who suffer the punishment of eternal fire.

Old Testament Law
Leviticus 18:22, 29
Do not have sexual relations with a man as one does with a woman; that is detestable... Everyone who does any of these detestable things – such people must be cut off from their people.

Other detestable sexual practices in that chapter: with mother, sister, daughter, granddaughter etc, with woman during period, with animal.

Leviticus 20:13
Same verse repeated, death penalty incurred

Other prohibitions in Leviticus: eating rabbit and pork 11:6-7, shellfish 11:1; wearing mixed fibres 19:19; working on the Sabbath 23:3, blasphemy 24:14

New Testament reactions to the law:
Matthew 5:17
[Jesus said] *'Do not think that I have come to abolish the law or the prophets; I have not come to abolish them but to fulfil them.'*

Acts 11:4-17
Peter's vision – told to eat 'unclean food'. Saw the gospel was for Gentiles: *'If God gave them the same gift he gave us who believed in the Lord Jesus Christ, who was I to think that I could stand in God's way?'*

Romans 10:4
Christ is the culmination of the law so that there may be righteousness for everyone who believes.

Galatians 5:4,13
You who are trying to be justified by the law have been alienated from Christ; you have fallen away from grace... You, my brothers and sisters, were called to be free. But do not use your freedom to indulge the flesh; rather serve one another in love.

Hebrews 8:8-13
The days are coming, declares the Lord, when I will make a new covenant ... By calling this covenant 'new' he has made the first one obsolete; and what is obsolete and outdated will soon disappear.

Old Testament Cult Prostitution
Deuteronomy 23:17
No Israelite man or woman is to become a shrine prostitute.

King James Version
There shall be no whore of the daughters of Israel, nor sodomite of the sons of Israel.

Also 1 Kings 14:24, 1 Kings 15:12, 1 Kings 22:46, 2 Kings 23:7

New Testament Immorality Lists
Romans 1:25-27
They [Godless people] *exchanged the truth about God for a lie, and worshipped and served created things rather than the Creator... Because of this, God gave them over to shameful lusts. Even their women exchanged natural sexual relations for unnatural ones. In the same way the men also abandoned natural relations with women and were inflamed with lust for one another. Men committed shameful acts with other men, and received in themselves the due penalty for their error.*

Other characteristics: Romans 1:29-31 *They have become filled with every kind of wickedness, evil, greed and depravity. They are full of envy, murder, strife, deceit and malice. They are gossips, slanderers, God-haters, insolent, arrogant and boastful ... they disobey their parents, they have no understanding, no fidelity, no mercy.*

1 Corinthians 6:9
Do you not know that wrongdoers will not inherit the kingdom of God? Do not be deceived: Neither the sexually immoral, nor idolaters nor adulterers nor men who have sex with men* nor thieves nor the greedy nor drunkards nor slanderers nor swindlers will inherit the kingdom of God.

1 Timothy 1:9-10
We know that the law is made not for the righteous but for lawbreakers and rebels, the ungodly and sinful, the unholy and irreligious, for those who kill their fathers or mothers, for murderers, for the sexually immoral, for those practising homosexuality*, for slave traders and liars and perjurers – and for whatever else is contrary to sound doctrine.

Celibacy
Matthew 19:10-12
[Jesus said] *'I tell you that anyone who divorces his wife, except for sexual immorality, and marries another woman commits adultery'. The disciples said to him, 'If this is the situation between a husband and a wife, it is better not to marry.' Jesus replied, 'Not everyone can accept this word, but only those to whom it has been given. For there are eunuchs who were born that way,*

---

*Literal Greek: *malakoi* – 'softies' and *arsenokoitai* – 'man in bed' i.e.: passive and active partners *eunuchs who have been made eunuchs by others – and there are those who choose to live like eunuchs for the sake of the kingdom of heaven. The one who can accept this should accept this.'*

1 Corinthians 7:8, 32-33, 38
Now to the unmarried and the widows I say: it is good for them to stay unmarried as I do. But if they cannot control themselves, they should marry, for it is better to marry than burn with passion ... An unmarried man is concerned about the Lord's affairs – how he can please the Lord. But a married man is concerned about the affairs of the world, how he can please his wife... So then, he who marries the virgin does right, but he who does not marry her does better.

Some key principles
Matthew 7:1
[Jesus said] *'Do not judge, or you too will be judged'*

Matthew 7:15-20
[Jesus said] *'By your fruits shall you know them'*

Matthew 25:35
[Jesus said] *'I was a stranger and you welcomed me in'*

John 8:7
Jesus said to them, 'Let any of you who is without sin be the first to throw a stone...'

Galatians 3:26-29
You are all children of God ... You are all one in Christ Jesus

Ephesians 2:8
For it is by grace that you have been saved, through faith – and this is not of yourselves, it is the gift of God;

Ephesians 4:15
Speaking the truth in love, we must grow up in every way into him

James 1:19
Everyone should be quick to listen, slow to speak and slow to become angry

1 John 4:18
Perfect love casts out fear

APPENDIX 3

Some recommended resources

BOOKS

'Permanent, Faithful, Stable': Christian Same-sex Marriage, Jeffrey John. (1993. 2nd edition 2012). Short book advocating same-sex marriage.

Journeys in Grace and Truth: Revisiting Scripture and Spirituality, Jayne Ozanne, ed. (2016). Short collection of essays by pro-gay Christians.

Washed and Waiting: Reflections on Christian Faithfulness and Homosexuality, Wesley Hill (2010). Viewpoint of gay evangelical who has chosen celibacy.

Satisfaction Guaranteed, Jonathan Berry with Rob Wood (2016). Suggests God can compensate those who resist same-sex temptation.

God and the Gay Christian, Matthew Vines (2014). In support of same-sex relationships, good on historical context.

Just Love: A Journey of Self-acceptance, Jayne Ozanne (2018). Autobiography by a prominent gay Anglican.

Undivided: Coming Out, Becoming Whole and Living Free From Shame, Vicky Beeching (2018). Autobiography of influential evangelical singer-songwriter who came out as gay in 2014.

ONLINE

The Bible and Homosexuality Part 1, Steve Chalk. Article by leading evangelical explaining his move to a pro-gay stance: http://www.premierchristianity. com/Featured-Topics/Homosexuality/The-Bible-and-Homosexuality-Part-One

The Bible and Homosexuality Part 2, Greg Downes. Article in response, from the traditionally evangelicalview:http://www.premierchristianity.com/ Featured-Topics/Homosexuality/The-Bible-and-Homosexuality-Part-Two

Homosexuality: Nature or Nurture, Dr Christopher L Heffner (2014). Good overview of nature v nurture debate. http://allpsych.com/journal/homosexuality/

Marriage and same-sex relationships
Church of England House of Bishops Report 2017.https:// www.churchofengland.org/media/3863472/gs-2055-marriage-and-same-sex-relationships-after-the-shared-conversations-report-from-the-house-of-bishops.pdf

Meanings of the Greek word 'arsenokotai'
More detailed analysis of relevant New Testament passages. http://www.religioustolerance.org/homarsen.htm

DVD

For the Bible tells me so, Dir: Daniel Carslake (2007) 98 mins. Stories of gay Christians and how their Christian parents came to terms with their orientation.

Broken, Writer: Jimmy McGovern (2017), six-part TV series. Drama about a priest in a tough Liverpool parish. Episode 5, where a devout homophobic uncle and a gay neighbour clash as they grieve over a teenage boy's death, would make a great discussion starter.